# A Slice of Tennessee

## US 70 by bicycle

# Bill Horner

© 2011 Bill Horner.  All rights reserved.
ISBN  978-1-257-89584-7

*For Marcia, Barry, and the people of Tennessee*

**Table of Contents**

*Acknowledgments*   vii

*Preface*   ix

Chapter 1   "We're on our way, Old Lady!"   1

Chapter 2   North Carolina State Line to Newport   5
            "I've been here before!"

Chapter 3   Newport to Knoxville   13
            Not the Tour de France

Chapter 4   Knoxville to Kingston   23
            Three Grand Divisions, Two Capitals, and One Long Steep Upgrade

Chapter 5   Kingston to Crossville   33
            Downhill to Memphis!

Chapter 6   Crossville to Smithville   41
            Serendipities

Chapter 7   Smithville to Lebanon   57
            A Character Counts

Chapter 8   Lebanon to Nashville   71
            New and Old

Chapter 9   Goodbye to an Old Friend   91

Chapter 10    Nashville to Dickson   95
          A Ninety-Degree Bend in the Road

Chapter 11    Dickson to Camden   113
          Roots and Wings

Chapter 12    Camden to Jackson   127
          Agriculture & Commerce

Chapter 13    Jackson to Memphis: Part I   143
          Southern Tradition

Chapter 14    Jackson to Memphis: Part II   157
          Southern Tradition

*Epilogue   The After-glow*   169

# Acknowledgments

"Hey, Rider!" Marcia's voice over the cell phone conveyed warmth and support audible even over the roar of the eighteen-wheelers traversing the Old Bridge in Memphis. In my excitement over crossing my self-imposed goal line, I paused to call Marcia back in East Tennessee to tell her I'd made it, that I'd met my goal, even as an old man (well, a 56-year-old). How good to have my better half encouraging me to realize my do-able dream. She gave up many an afternoon driving around, browsing nursery or antique shops or just being bored while her husband racked up miles on his adventure.

I love the word *excellent.* It connotes more than just quality—it also communicates creativity, discipline, initiative, discernment, and a host of other desirable attributes. Add one or two *!!*'s after it, and it gives the spirits a major boost. Early in my trans-state endeavor, my old high school buddy Barry Chamberlain bestowed such an *Excellent!!* on me when I informed him by email of my two-wheeled project. He began sending out my periodic write-ups on the ride to other friends. By the time I reached Jackson, Barry was up from Houston to pedal alongside me to Memphis and the finish. Without his encouragement I might not have finished the ride, certainly not this book.

Don't you just love those individuals that reach for the stars—and sometimes manage to grab hold of them? Lon Chenowith, my long-time colleague in the ministry, has grabbed a few in his lifetime. His section hike of the Appalachian Trail from Springer Mountain, Georgia, to Mt. Katahdin, Maine—and his book chronicling the 14-year endeavor—inspired me to my own do-able dream of bike riding the state of Tennessee. He is currently doing a section bike ride of his own—from Canada to Mexico along the western Continental Divide.

On Day One of my adventure, still damp from my wet ride, I appealed to Editor Rick Hooper of *The Newport Plain Talk* newspaper to publish my write-up of the first leg of the Ride. He graciously ran my feature—complete with picture—in the Sunday edition. Such attention so early on added a sense of legitimacy to my dream.

The Knoxville Journal and The News-Herald (in Loudon County) each ran my write-up of the Ride through their respective regions. Their interest increased my own excitement and passion for this project.

J. R. Lind of The Lebanon Democrat projected an almost electric enthusiasm on a cold and exhausting October day as I pedaled past the office of this fine newspaper. J. R. wrote up a feature story on the Ride that was—well— excellent!!

Thanks to Rev. Jonas Taylor and his wife Colleen for treating me to dinner in Lebanon. They are gracious servants of the Lord.

And a special thanks to Les and Jaynee Bodansky for their abundant hospitality to two tired, sweaty bike riders who had no other options for a night's lodging. This delightful couple's gracious generosity transformed a bed and breakfast into a family fellowship experience.

Many other friends, relatives, and strangers showed genuine interest and provided needed encouragement along the way to inspire this naïve senior citizen to realize a dream.

# Preface

Tennessee.  It comes from the name of a Cherokee town in what is now Monroe County.  It means possibly "winding river," "meeting place," or "river of the great bend."  Founded in 1796 after a false start as the state of Franklin, Tennessee would become home to a rich history and numerous colorful characters, including explorer James Robertson, settler and Revolutionary War hero John Sevier, Texas heroes Davy Crockett and Sam Houston, and three presidents of the United States, Andrew Jackson, James Knox Polk, and Andrew Johnson.  Tennessee would earn the moniker *The Volunteer State* due to the record number of young men who volunteered to serve during the War of 1812. General Andrew Jackson led many of these volunteers in a rout of the British regulars at New Orleans at the end of that war, preventing the British from taking control of the Mississippi River.

This same state has shown remarkable resilience through the years.  It weathered the major earthquake that formed Reelfoot Lake.  It survived a war for southern independence that tore apart the state as well as the nation.  The Great Depression hit hard but left a series of TVA dams and Civilian Conservation Corps-built parks in its wake.  In more recent times, tornadoes have ravaged numerous towns, and flooding recently destroyed a large part of Nashville in what is perhaps the worst non-hurricane disaster in our nation's history.  But Tennessee has always rebounded.

This is the state I love.

And this bicycle ride was about reconnecting with the state while making new discoveries.  The resultant book is not a travelogue but the record of a pilgrimage, the chronicle of a senior citizen's do-able dream, the narrative of an encounter with the Tennessee that has so shaped my life.

The Ride unfolded in unexpected ways.  Originally I planned to do a series of city-to-city trips, such as Knoxville to Nashville and Jackson to

Memphis.  But once born, the idea took on a whole life of its own.  The challenge of US 70 from the North Carolina line to the Mississippi River at Memphis was alluring.  And after the first day's ride, I spotted *The Newport Plain Talk* newspaper office, and suddenly writing about the riding became almost as important as the riding itself.  The earlier rides were shorter one day affairs, on my day off from work.  Later rides required vacation days and were longer, with more frequent stops and adventures.  I even took more pictures as the Ride progressed.  And the quality of the pictures improved west of Crossville, when I finally replaced my old worn out camera that wouldn't even focus anymore with a new reliable one.  The chapters of this book reflect that progression.

Along the way I encountered:

13 riding days

9 fabulous dry rub ribs at Rendevous Restaurant

5 major river crossings

5 ducks marching down the red carpet at the Peabody Hotel

4 old steel truss bridges (near Newport, Donelson, Smithville, and Memphis)

4 newspaper articles on the Ride

4 still functional drive-in theaters

4 flat tires

4 seasons

3 Grand Divisions of Tennessee

3 state capitals (Knoxville, Kingston, and Nashville)

3 bulls, outside the fence, one stepping out into the highway

3 riding partners

2 bicycles

2 cameras

2 miniature-but-still-big Statues of Liberty

Many new friends

Dozens of bottles of Gatorade and water

Hundreds of pictures

Thousands of memories

And ONE FANTASTIC STATE!


And now to the book.  Enjoy the Ride!

xii

# Chapter 1  "We're on our way, Old Lady!"

I am not a native of Tennessee. But that is an accident of birth. I got here as quickly as I could. Tennessee is my home. Although I have lived many places, the Lord always seems to bring me back here. Other states have a charm and beauty all their own, but I would rather live here than anywhere else on earth.

How did a transplant come to love the state so much? Maybe it was the culture shock of 1962, when Dad was transferred from our home in a flat, bland-looking area near the coast to hilly, colorful Knoxville. At age nine I experienced for the first time the wonder of four seasons: the color and brisk air of fall, the beauty and fun of winter snowfalls, the dogwood and azalea blossoms of spring, and the warm green leafy days of summer. East Tennesseans were some of the friendliest people I had ever encountered, as evidenced by the ever-present "Are ye alright?" greeting. The proximity of Gatlinburg and Cades Cove didn't hurt.

*A Slice of Tennessee*

However it happened, Tennessee wormed its way into my heart. Ironically, though, both schooling and the ministry have required that I live in numerous other places outside the state for most of my adult life. Only recently have I been able to relocate back in Tennessee. I arrived with a burning desire to experience the state afresh. So one Friday in late September, at age fifty-five, I loaded my bicycle onto the back of my pick-up, my wife by my side, and headed toward Newport and the Tennessee/North Carolina state line. The spark of a dream in my heart was about to burst into open flame. I would bike my way across the state of Tennessee on Highway US 70. This dream was my leap over the mid-life crisis, a means of warding off old age for at least several more months. This ride was not for the purpose of raising awareness of (or money for) some worthy cause. It would not be a race. *Guinness Book of World Records* could have no interest in what I was doing. No, this ride was for the pure, wholesome pleasure of it, a chance to experience what God has given us richly to enjoy: the privilege of living in Tennessee.

The inspiration for this adventure came from multiple sources. Television personality Art Linkletter and author Mark Victor Hansen (*Chicken Soup for the Soul*) in their book *How to Make the Rest of Your Life the Best of Your Life* recommend accepting new challenges to keep active in mind and body in the senior years. This ride would certainly be such a challenge. And my close pastor friend Dr. Lon Chenowith spurred me on by his example. Over a fourteen year period Lon traversed the entire Appalachian Trail from Springer Mountain, Georgia, to Mt. Katahdin, Maine. A section hiker, Lon would spend a week or two of vacation time annually out on the trail. I could accomplish this dream in sections, too. And finally, Peter Jenkins's *A Walk across America* and *The Walk West* held me spellbound, as he chronicled his journey the length and breadth of this land. I was itching to get out on the road.

Unfortunately my great adventure did not begin with the bang I expected. That first day everything seemed to go wrong. The "chance of a passing shower" quickly turned into an all day rain. I got a late start. I would have to finish early because Marcia had to travel to Nashville later in the day to

*Chapter 1 "We're on our way, Old Lady!"*

visit her ailing father. And on the ninety minute drive from our house to the state line, I had to make two bathroom stops (nervous excitement?). Before the day was over I could add a flat tire and a broken spoke to my woes.

As we arrived at the state line, the do-nothing option was looking more and more attractive. The only activity around the border was a bar and a convenience store with the cleanest public bathroom I'd ever seen (my third stop that morning). Mike at the store told me his family had owned the business and the building next door for decades. He was a North Carolina man. I told him of my plans for riding the state. He showed polite interest but must have wondered what would possess a man with a perfectly good pick-up to bike in the chilly rain.

Actor Gene Kelly sang and danced in the rain. Neil Sedaka sang of the laughter he could hear in the rain. I didn't feel like singing or dancing, but I could imagine a lot of laughter from anyone who saw me out pedaling in the precipitation.

The moment of decision came. "I feel like an idiot either way," I despaired to Marcia. "Riding in the rain seems just plain silly. But if we turn back now, we've driven all the way up here for nothing." I could always try it again the next week. But I could feel the dream beginning to slip away. Hadn't Lon told me he had experienced days just like this one out on the trail—driving rain, snow literally up to his knees at times? Drawing a deep breath, I pulled on my rain poncho and began to unload my bike. But then I couldn't get the hold down bolt on the bike rack loose. It was too wet. The socket wrench kept slipping. I had to go back inside and ask Mike for a half-inch wrench. Mike was obliging, and in no time, I had freed up my bike. Now that excuse was gone. I asked Marcia to take a picture of me next to the state line sign, just in case I could indeed pull off this dream. I was so rattled I forgot to include my bike in the photo. Finally, despite mounting trepidation, I began pedaling toward Newport in the rain. Even the dogs along the highway had enough sense to stay inside.

But a bicycle is a strange and wonderful vehicle. Within minutes my Diamondback Crestview began to work its magic. Even in the chilly drizzle my dampened spirit and the cares and stresses of life were melting away. Such woes just cannot cling to the back of a man on a bicycle. Suddenly I was no longer an idiot. No, I was the luckiest man in Tennessee. The sounds of the rushing river, the smells of rain-soaked forest and open air sawmills, the sights of wild turkeys and fog-shrouded mountains are so vivid in the open air at bicycle speed. I was getting soaked to the skin despite my poncho, but it no longer mattered. I had made the right decision. "We're on our way, Old Lady!" I planned to tell Marcia. One of Charles Dickens's characters in *Our Mutual Friend* made such an exclamation of delight to his wife as they began to acquire some book-learning in their old age. Marcia is not old by any means and is quite attractive. Nevertheless the line brought me pleasure. The ride had begun. I was finally on my way!

**Worth the ride even in the rain**

# Chapter 2  North Carolina State Line to Newport
## "I've been here before!"

How many times had I been down this road before? Dozens, at least. But nothing looked familiar. Not that I wasn't enjoying the ride. I was, even in the rain.

US 70 from the North Carolina line to Newport runs off a mountain, then follows the narrow valley floor along the French Broad River. So the grades were not too steep and were mostly downhill on this stretch. While the shoulder was quite narrow, the traffic was light. These factors combined to make for an enjoyable ride. Besides, I knew where I could purchase some good dry clothes cheap in Newport at the end of the ride.

To my left across the highway and the river, massive mountain ridges loomed above me. Dollops of fog hung here and there on the slopes. The schoolteacher Christy in the classic novel of the same name could look out her bedroom window in the Cocke County mission house and see fourteen mountain ranges. I felt something of her wonder now. But why could I not remember it from my childhood? On the many weekend trips our family made from Knoxville to my grandmother's house in Hendersonville, North Carolina, we had often traversed this route.

I spied some broken pavement in the woods which might partially explain my memory loss. A kink in the road had been straightened, the remains of the old route long since so overgrown with trees that one might miss it at car speed—but not at bicycle speed. How could I remember sights that had been so altered over time?

The Del Rio post office was obviously a new building. Nothing to remember there. How, I wondered, did the local residents ever come up with a Spanish name for a small town tucked away in a corner of Cocke County with its Scotch-Irish roots? Originally named Big Creek, the town experienced problems in the 1800's as postal service improved. It seems there was another Big Creek, Tennessee. Their solution to the inevitable mix-ups was to change their name. Del Rio is Spanish for "by the river." Had it not been so wet, I might have pedaled the mile or so into Del Rio to see the place with my own eyes. Could there possibly be any Mexican restaurants there?

I continued to pedal and dig deep into the recesses of my memory. Surely I should remember the distinctive old truss bridge where the highway finally intersected the river. It was named for Major J. T. Huff. Does anyone remember the Major? I had better remember his namesake bridge quickly—a partially-built reinforced concrete successor was champing at the bit to take over for the tired old structure. But once again, in the language of nearby Del Rio, the whole scene registered *nada* among my childhood impressions. This was not the only bridge worth remembering on this route, either. Downriver could be seen a many-decades old railroad bridge supported by high, strong trestles. An equally dated bridge over little Laurel Creek had significantly large concrete side rails. And a bridge ushering travelers into Newport was adorned with colorful flowers arranged in baskets on its side rails.

*Chapter 2    North Carolina State Line to Newport*

**Not too many steel truss bridges left on US 70**

Because of the rain and a broken spoke (and Marcia's trip later that day to Nashville), it seemed prudent to cut this ride short. Newport, not Dandridge, would be the end of the line on this day. That was still a good twenty mile ride. The miles slid by in no time. Despite the rocky start and the wet, chilly weather, I was thoroughly enjoying the journey. This Tennessee riding project held out the prospect of being a fabulous adventure.

Too soon the outskirts of Newport began to pass by. Traffic picked up, surprisingly heavy for such a small town. The rain held most people indoors. But one grizzled old laborer was standing in a parking lot as I pedaled by, flashing a toothy grin and giving me a big thumbs up. Well, at least one other person on the planet didn't think I was crazy.

My memory suddenly began working again as I entered the town proper but not because of recollections from my childhood. Rather it was a trip to the town about ten years earlier with the late Norman Gary Hughes that stirred up

*A Slice of Tennessee*

old impressions now. Norman grew up in Newport. A loyal, dedicated, and intelligent man, he served as a deacon in the church I pastored in Bristol at that time. His friendship and support were dear to me because of his origin. I had always heard that Cocke Countians were known for being clannish, that they did not open up to strangers easily or trust outsiders. Norman had little to say, but he proved to be as loyal a friend as I ever had. I cherished such support during a church ministry that had been quite stressful.

Warm memories now flooded in. Every Thursday night back in Bristol, Norman would accompany me to make ministry visits. He knew many local people that I did not. On one particularly stormy Thursday, the local radio station broadcast a tornado warning while we were driving around in my 1969 Ford F150 truck looking for an address. I could see that the storm was worrying my big friend. "Brother Bill, I think we better head back to the church," he urged. Knowing what a die-hard Ford man he was, I couldn't help myself. "Norman, are you afraid a tornado might hurt a Ford truck?" I asked. He considered his answer carefully. "Well. . . it might tear off some of the trim."

One warm summer Thursday evening, Norman and I had paired off with two other men for visiting, going in different directions. Another church member named Mike and I, riding in my old Ford truck, encountered a dead skunk in an elderly gentleman's driveway. One tire must have hit the unfortunate critter. But the deceased skunk had the last laugh. Who would have known it could still impart such a stink. The pungent odor followed us to our next visit and all the way back to the church. Norman and others standing in the church parking lot were holding their noses when we were still fifty yards away. That dead skunk haunted my truck for days. The next Sunday after church I discovered that someone had put a small black-and-white item on the old Ford's side view mirror—a cute little skunk Beanie Baby. I knew who the culprit was, for Norman's wife collected those things. I still have it.

I had hoped to live and minister in Bristol for many years, but the Lord sometimes leads us around unexpected ninety degree bends in this life. A church in Maryland approached me to be their pastor, and I felt compelled to

*Chapter 2    North Carolina State Line to Newport*

go. Leaving our home on the hill in Bristol, however, was difficult for Marcia and me. It made matters worse that after several fruitless months we were still trying to sell the house. When I returned to town briefly to do some painting and fixing up, Norman showed up dressed to work, a sack of sandwiches in hand from the local barbecue stand (he knew I loved them). A true friend.

One Saturday in 1998 just prior to our move to Maryland, Norman drove me down to Newport to introduce me to his old stomping grounds. He still owned property, left him by his late parents. Our first stop, however, was to Brock's store, where we purchased Philly cheesesteak sandwiches. How the locals in Newport ever learned to cook this famous delight invented in Philadelphia I'll never know. No microwaving there—they cooked the beef on a griddle and then added every topping imaginable. I have been to Philadelphia and dined on a Philly cheesesteak sandwich at one of the two restaurants that claim to have invented the culinary masterpiece. But it was not as good (or as messy, the true measure of a gourmet sandwich) as the one they fixed me at Brock's. On our way out Norman purchased a large roll of paper towels for us to use as napkins—we needed them.

Our next stop on that memorable trip was Newport Dry Goods Store. Norman's intention in bringing me to town that day was to buy me a new suit there. Our first order of business was to meet the proprietor, Carroll Kyker. Mr. Kyker had been Norman's supervisor when he had worked there during his high school years. "How did you come to work here?" I asked Norman. (Somehow Norman did not seem the dry goods type to me.) Norman shrugged and replied, "Well. . . when I was sixteen, I was walking down the sidewalk in front of the store. One of the clerks stopped me and said, 'You're a big boy. Would you like to earn a little money this afternoon helping us move some goods downstairs?' I looked at her, shrugged, and said, 'O.K.' And I worked there the next two years." It seemed so typically Norman.

As we stepped outside with our purchases in hand, I looked up and down the block and across the street toward the railroad track. I had the distinct feeling that I had been on that street before. Suddenly it dawned on

*A Slice of Tennessee*

me. Some childhood memories at last began to resurface. I had indeed been on this block before, not once but several times. But I had come in a different way. "Norman!" I said excitedly, "I've been here before. I used to ride through here sometimes on the train when I was a boy!" Big, quiet Norman pondered that revelation. "Well. . .," he asked, "why didn't you wave?"

In the mid 1960's Southern Railway still ran a passenger train from Knoxville to Columbia, South Carolina. I would ride it on occasion to visit my grandmother in Hendersonville, North Carolina. The view of Tennessee by train is quite different from the view by highway. It affords a look at the back side of numerous towns, as well as valleys, rivers, and bridges not seen along any highway. But I was always intrigued by the town with the store fronts facing the train track and shoppers scurrying here and there. It seemed as if the train were traveling down main street. I did not know at the time what town it was. But standing on that street decades later with Norman, it all came together.

And now here I was back in Newport again, this time by bicycle. After linking up with Marcia, my ride now officially over for the day, we stopped at Newport Dry Goods Store again. Wet as I was, I thought it looked heavenly. The extra clothes I had judiciously packed along with me that morning (short pants and a T-shirt) seemed woefully inadequate for such a chilly, wet day. Besides, I had no dry underwear or socks. Wet clothes are almost tolerable except for soaked socks inside waterlogged shoes—they render the whole outfit miserable. But in the store I found casual pants, a shirt, socks, underwear, and even a cheap pair of athletic shoes for a total of $33. Laying my purchases on the counter, I asked the clerk for permission to change into them in the dressing room, then just wear them out of the store. She agreed but gave me that puzzled look I would encounter again and again on my unusual ride across the state. No matter—it was wonderful just to be dry again! Good dry clothes from Newport Dry Goods.

Before departing town, we stopped at Brock's and got sandwiches for lunch (Philly cheesesteak for me). They were as messy and delicious as ever. Then we proceeded down Main Street (US 70) through quaint, single-head four-

*Chapter 2   North Carolina State Line to Newport*

sided traffic lights that I honestly remember from childhood. Arriving at the office of *The Newport Plain Talk* newspaper, I excitedly related my adventure to Managing Editor Rick Hooper. He listened graciously as I expressed my desire to write up the day's experiences as a news feature for his publication.  He encouraged me to submit it.  They ran the story, complete with a picture of me standing with my bicycle between a Ford truck and the railroad tracks.

**An interesting town—by train, Ford truck, or bicycle**

It's funny how history, even personal history, repeats itself. On all those trips through Newport as a boy, both by highway and by railroad, I could not have guessed that one day I would be entering the town and exiting one of those stores with such a good supportive friend as Norman, he my deacon, I his pastor.  Nor could I have imagined that still later I would be revisiting these same locations yet again—but this time by bicycle.  So maybe I remembered more than I originally thought. And maybe this ride across Tennessee would truly be a memory-filled adventure.

**19.45 miles for the day**

**19.45 miles total**

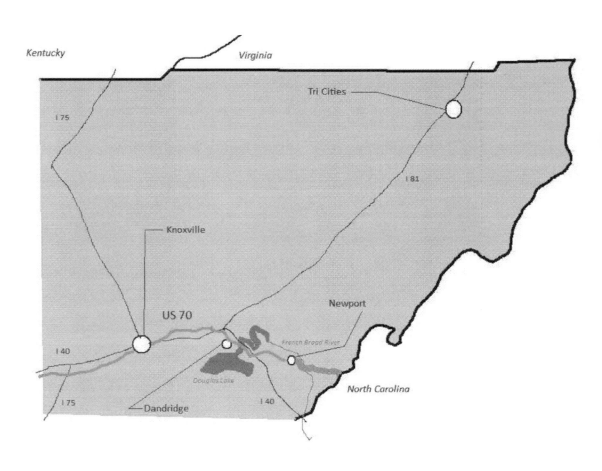

# Chapter 3  Newport to Knoxville
# Not the Tour de France

I was back on the road after only one week. It was my day off, a warm sunny inviting Friday early in October. Marcia had agreed to drop me off in Newport. My goal that day was to pedal through Dandridge and on into Knoxville by mid-afternoon. The dream was alive. I was feeling good. US 70 was beckoning. There were plenty of steep hills on this route. The original plan had been a twenty-five mile stretch. However, since rain had cut my first ride short, I would have to cover about forty-five miles this day, still manageable even with time to stop and smell the roses.


I am not Lance Armstrong. I am not in a hurry. I ride a moderately heavy hybrid bicycle with old fashioned turned up handlebars and a nice, large, thick-padded seat. Multiple gears are acceptable, twenty-four of them to be exact, but they are for steep grades, not speed. If time were a factor, I'd get on I-40 in a fast car. This endeavor was not the Tour de France. The journey would

*A Slice of Tennessee*

ultimately take me to Memphis and the Mississippi River, but it was not a race. There were East Tennessee hills and trees and clear blue autumn skies to view and enjoy. Tennessee holds many delights for the tourist or native traveling through the state. On the right road on the right day at the right speed, one might experience colorful local culture and history, farm animals, exhilarating fall scenery, steep hills and narrow hollers so characteristic of East Tennessee, and—if you were fortunate enough to have been raised here—a deep well of long-forgotten memories. There was so much Tennessee to be discovered or rediscovered in the open air at bicycle speed. How much had I missed so many times by auto at interstate speed?

Pedaling over the long, high bridge over the French Broad River (Douglas Lake), I could view the mountains and water as if suspended in mid-air. Crossing large bodies of water is always exciting on a bicycle. I was approaching Dandridge, the second-oldest city in Tennessee. Incorporated in 1783 as the county seat of Jefferson County, it is a junior town only to Jonesborough. The name always intrigued me as a child, I think because it sounded like "Drainage." However, that name may be appropriate, considering that much of the downtown is below the high-water mark of nearby Douglas Dam on the French Broad River. Indeed, upon construction of the dam in 1942, the townsfolk appealed to First Lady Eleanor Roosevelt to spare the central business district from the onslaught of floodwater. Their argument? It just wouldn't be right to flood historic French Broad Baptist Church. The church, founded in 1781, was one of the oldest in Tennessee. According to Wilma Dykeman in her work *The French Broad,* one church member, Cousin Fanny (Mrs. Alfred Swann), "in pale silk and chiffon, turned her pen and ink against the yards of concrete mixing in the hoppers. She wrote letters to Senators, and sent poems to the President's wife." And it didn't hurt that this was also the only town in the nation named after the *wife* of first president George Washington—Martha *Dandridge* Washington. The First Lady was persuaded, exercised her influence, and the

*Chapter 3   Newport to Knoxville*

Tennessee Valley Authority constructed a levee parallel to Main Street behind the town proper.

But the history of this area actually goes back even further. Many years prior to the arrival of either the dam or the first white settlers, a Native American chiefdom called *Chiaha* existed on Zimmerman's Island in the French Broad River near here. Spanish explorers Hernando de Soto and Juan Pardo visited the area in the mid 1500's. A leap of three hundred years would find Confederate General Longstreet's and Union General Ambrose Burnside's forces clashing briefly in this area over control of the city of Knoxville. Still later the town would be home to prominent businessman Alfred Austell, founder of a large cotton brokerage.

All of that history is well and good, and I am sure the above individuals contributed much to the lore of Dandridge. But this writer (rider) has always been far more impressed with the community's colorful storyteller, the late Bert Vincent. In the 1960's Mr. Vincent's "Strolling" column in *The Knoxville News-Sentinel* was the first item other than the comics page of any newspaper that I ever read on a regular basis. His tales held me spellbound.

In one of his yarns, some mountain good ole boys got to arguing about how long a man could hang and still live. One of them bet the others a barrel of whiskey he could hang two full minutes. They took the bet. But barely did they have him hoisted when a really swell dog fight broke out down the hill. The boys only remembered their hanging buddy three or four minutes later. When they cut him loose, he could barely whisper. "You won the whiskey!" they told him sympathetically. "But I can't drink it!" he rasped back.

Mr. Vincent also related the story of the creepy Middle Tennessee Bell Witch, who even stirred the curiosity of Andrew Jackson. Another especially hair-raising tale was the disappearance of David Lang. It seems that farmer Lang was out working one of his fields when company came to call. Lang turned toward the house and waved, took a step or two, and suddenly vanished before their eyes. No sinkhole or any other plausible explanation presented itself. He was just gone, never to be seen again. (Some say the whole story was a hoax concocted by others, but it sure gave this young reader chills and thrills.)

Once, ole Bert encountered Minnie Pearl at a ramp festival. (For the uninitiated, ramps are East Tennessee-grown wild herbs with onion-like bulbs and garlic-like flavor.) There was a picture in his column of him and Minnie feeding each other the strong leeks. And in another column he told of a dry cleaning store clerk in Knoxville who found a tarantula in the parking lot of his establishment. That store was only a mile or so from my house!

And now I was nearing old Bert's town. He would have been intrigued by all the interesting sights I encountered that day near his old stomping grounds. For instance, on the outskirts of the city, I pedaled to the top of a rise and found myself face to face with a huge brown bull. Not liking the way he was eyeing me, I passed around him on the opposite side of the road. He was entering the traffic lane as I pedaled past him. For all I know he may be quarter-pounders by now. Two of his massive buddies were standing a few feet distant in a driveway watching. Thankfully I was wearing orange, not red. I don't believe I have ever encountered a real live bull on I-40.

**I gave him the right-of-way!**

*Chapter 3   Newport to Knoxville*

One farm I passed on the right was full of rock outcroppings.  I could not imagine trying to push a plow through that field.  Yet someone once obviously had.  They had earned their living (perhaps still did) off that rocky land.  I was going to stop and take a picture but declined since the lady of the house was outside watching the strange character on the bicycle.  A little further down the highway, I rode past a young woman sitting at a red light at a cross street in town.  She didn't think I was strange.  Rather she urged me on with a big smile and a hearty, "Pedal faster!  Pedal faster!"

A roadside sign advertised a local bail bondsman.  What was puzzling was the layout of the ad.  It included a large cartoon drawing of Betty Boop.  I am still trying to figure out her connection to the legal system in Jefferson County, Tennessee.  Miss Boop does not seem to fit the local profile.  A convenience store clerk down the highway near Kodak would come closer.  In need of fuel (I average 150 mpgg, miles per gallon of Gatorade), I stepped up to the counter to make a purchase.

"That'll be a dollar forty. . .," the clerk began.  Suddenly she caught herself and started over.  "Are ye alright?"  What a delightful greeting!  I came to love it as a boy in Knoxville but had not heard it much in recent years.  Only after I assured her that indeed I was alright thank-you did she reveal the full dollar forty-nine price of my drink.

Many more miles up and down hills would bring me to the outskirts of Knoxville.  Rounding a bend at the junction of my highway with US 11E, I spotted a favorite Horner family haunt of yesteryear on the left.  In the 1960's the restaurant was called *Helma's,* and it served a wide variety of delectable dishes.  Adding to the culinary delight was the live organ music, played with vigor by a local woman sitting near the large front plate glass window.  I don't know to this day how I did it, but as we were leaving there one evening with happy tummys, I somehow tripped on the front walkway and fell right against that plate glass.  I didn't hurt anything (but my pride), but I sure startled the organist!  The entire restaurant clientele looked up from their meals.  The loud thump, followed by the most discordant chord they'd ever heard on any organ, added some extra spice to the dinner music that night. It is not *Helma's* anymore—the organist is probably gone, too.

My legs were getting fatigued. Forty miles and counting of steep grades was taking its toll. But I couldn't quit now. There was still too much to see. In fact, this stretch was the payoff. I was entering memory lane. I grew up in a modest but comfortable home just a few miles from here, and I knew the area well. Soon I was pedaling across the bridge over the Holston River. This bridge was obviously a replacement of an older steel truss structure. But it was the same river and the same spot that my pal Eddy Shoemaker and I had visited many times on our old cruiser bikes as young teenagers.

Eddy was as good a buddy as a young boy could have. We met in Mrs. Murray's fourth grade class at Chilhowee School on this same highway right after my family's move to Knoxville. Eddy was my first friend in the new and different culture into which I was thrust at age nine. He was afflicted with a disease of the leg called Perthes and had to hobble around on crutches for about three years. But he was more dexterous on crutches than most of us were on two good legs. Eddy was not afraid to attempt anything, and he had an imagination and an intellect to fuel that admirable mindset.

**Hasn't changed much since 1962**

*Chapter 3   Newport to Knoxville*

Once when we were walking down Holston Drive near my house, we encountered a green snake.  We managed to pick it up with a stick and get it home.  We named him Jerome and took turns keeping him (a month at Eddy's house, a month at my house).  Poor old Jerome had a problem—he was a little on the dead side.  We had preserved him in a jar of rubbing alcohol.  That kept him from rotting, but Eddy's mom soon got sick of looking at the creature and made him dispose of our serpentine pet.

Eddy always had the good ideas.  He found an ad in a comic book for hot air balloons.  He figured that four of them would have enough lift to get either him or me airborne.  The only thing that stood in our way was the money to buy them.  Alas, how many a scientist has been deterred by a similar lack of funding.

Once Eddy was off the crutches, our world enlarged somewhat, for he was able then to ride a bicycle.  Walking keeps adolescents on a short tether.  But with bikes we could visit that bridge on Asheville Highway (US 70) and throw rocks into the Holston River.  We would stand at the same spot from which a despondent man had once jumped to his death.  Eddy and I were convinced, however, that a successful jump was possible without bodily harm.  We planned to try it, with proper precautions of course.  Safety equipment would include wooden splints (to keep the legs from breaking when the jumper hit the water) and a good strong rope (so the helper could fish him out afterward).  But unfortunately that very summer Eddy's family moved to Atlanta.  Our promising plan went into the inactive file (where it remains to this day).

Eddy and I lost contact sometime in the 1970's.  But he had helped to broaden my horizons.  With him I discovered Jules Verne, Robert Mitchum, *The Long Ships, Shenandoah,* five cent cokes at Chilhowee Pharmacy, a funeral for a hamster (complete with *Rock of Ages* played on my violin), and yes, even that tarantula—in person—at  Holston Dry Cleaners that Bert Vincent had informed us of.  For years I wondered about my old friend.  But in 2004, through the marvel of the internet, we linked up again.  He lives back in Knoxville now.  He reminded me of a pact we made when he moved to Atlanta all those years ago:

*A Slice of Tennessee*

if ever we lost contact we would meet in June of the year 2000 at the Grand Canyon. Somehow we missed that rendezvous, but we now still meet occasionally for lunch. We still haven't scraped together the cash for those hot air balloons.


I biked past old Chilhowee, our elementary alma mater, which looked as stern and imposing as when I first met Eddy there in 1962. Then I made it as far as Chilhowee Park before a flat tire stopped me. How many a September I had ridden the rides, eaten the feeds, and played the games afforded by the Tennessee A & I Fair at this very park. No telling how many quarters I had wasted trying to ball pitch or ring toss my way to winning some cheesy prize. (I never won.) Older and wiser now, I rejected the challenge of riding on to downtown Knoxville. It took only minutes to fix the flat, but I decided to listen to my aching muscles. Forty-three miles of steep grades had taken enough toll for one day. But what a day it had been! The bright blue sky, the leaves reluctantly letting go their green color in favor of yellows and reds, and the warm Tennessee fall weather were worth every hill, every sore muscle. Marcia would be somewhere in the general vicinity. Indeed, she had had a good day as well, with her discoveries of two garden stores, a craft shop, and a number of friendly people. She appeared in no time to pick me up.

I now had two days of riding under my belt. I had traversed the North Carolina line to Knoxville. I was getting a little air under my wings and was beginning to fly. The next Friday would get me on to Kingston and perhaps beyond.

Thank God for interstate highways that get us places we need to go quickly. But thank Him also for the old byways that allow us to experience such a slice of Tennessee as I had that day, especially at bicycle speed. Lance Armstrong should try it.

*Chapter 3   Newport to Knoxville*

**If you're in a hurry**

**If you want to experience a slice of Tennessee**

*A Slice of Tennessee*

**43.28 miles for the day**

**62.73 miles total**

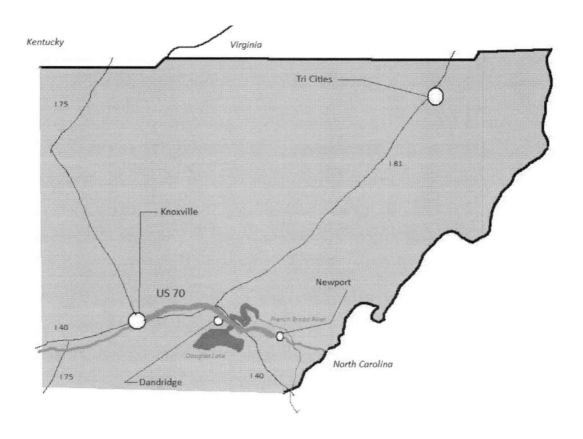

# Chapter 4  Knoxville to Kingston
# Three Grand Divisions, Two Capitals, and One Long Steep Upgrade

I was seeing a Tennessee I had known all my life and yet never experienced quite like this before.  The view is different along the old byways.  And at bicycle speed it all comes into sharp focus.  For the third Friday in a row I mounted my Diamondback Crestview and started down the highway.   As any Tennessee schoolchild knows, our state is comprised of three Grand Divisions: East, Middle, and West.  (I have always loved that expression *Grand Division*; it sounds so majestic!)  But on this forty-mile ride from Knoxville to Kingston I experienced a different set of grand divisions: big city, rural countryside, and small town.

Knoxville has definitely graduated to "big city" status.  As a child I often thought of it as an adolescent, overgrown small town.  But an ever-growing major university, vibrant commercial district, and a world's fair (1982), among other factors, have taken the town across the threshold of city adulthood.

*A Slice of Tennessee*

For this leg of my journey, I had Marcia drop me off at Chilhowee School, my elementary alma mater. I would overlap my previous week's ride by about half a mile, since my camera had malfunctioned earlier and I had wanted to snap a picture of the dear old schoolhouse. It's amazing how little schools and prisons change over the years. Conflicting emotions of contentment and dread resurfaced from my days there forty-plus years ago. Within those walls I forged lifelong friendships and numerous acquaintances. But I still tremble inside at the thought of the principal, Mrs. Freeman, standing in the cafeteria doorway shouting, "Alright! Alright! Let's get quiet in here!" with a look that *dared* anyone to resist.

My first day in Chilhowee School was in September of 1962. I was assigned to Mrs. Murray's fourth grade class in one of the oldest classrooms in this ancient edifice. The school had been constructed in 1928, with slave labor, I suspected. (My previous school in Florida had been a modern state-of-the-art structure.) I knew nobody, but they all knew each other. The teacher had me sitting up front. I was petrified. My loneliness only intensified when the class played "Seven Up" at recess, a game in which students had to guess who tapped them while their eyes were closed. How could I guess? I didn't even know their names.

But by a fortuitous whim of Mrs. Murray's seating re-arrangement, I soon found myself in the next-to-the-back seat, in front of a boy named Eddy. He asked me one morning what time it was, claimed he couldn't see the clock from his desk. (He later confessed he just couldn't tell time very well.) I informed him of the correct time, and the rest is history. As I described in the previous chapter, we became fast friends, partners in crime, kindred spirits. When Eddy's family moved to Atlanta four years later, we made our famous pact to meet in the year 2000 at the Grand Canyon (hey, we'd never seen it before!). Unfortunately, Y2K came and went without our grand reunion. When we crossed paths again in 2004, however, we agreed that if we ever lose contact again, we will meet at the Grand Canyon in 2025.

*Chapter 4    Knoxville to Kingston*

Chilhowee School soon fell behind as I continued biking through Knoxville. While Knoxville as a whole is quite hilly, this stretch of US 70 was relatively level. I welcomed the brief respite from the constant up-and-down.

History was made here. Established around 1786, this city was the capital of Tennessee until 1817. Personal history was made here, too. Proceeding along Asheville Highway toward downtown, I passed familiar sights: Dr. William Byrd's pediatric office was still there, though he is long retired. Dr. Byrd and his nurses Wanda and Gertie saw us through many a childhood illness. My older brother Rick once called on him when my great-grandmother suffered a stroke at our house. The personable pediatrician was only too glad to help with our geriatric crisis.

The huge Kay's Ice Cream cone was still in place, though the name had changed. Our family did its part to keep Kay's in business. A & P Food Store and Chilhowee Pharmacy were long gone. But the Pizza Palace was still the Pizza Palace.

It is amazing how quickly the miles pass in the city while reminiscing. In no time I had arrived at Gay Street in the heart of downtown Knoxville. Upon moving to the city in 1962, I discovered that my peers frequently spoke of going someplace called *uptown.* Just how far *up*town extends from *down*town I did not know, but they both seemed to meet on Gay Street. While this area's many stores, theaters, and businesses have changed much over the years, the avenue itself looks very much the same as it did decades ago. The huge old Tennessee Theater is now the scene of concerts, including everything from classical music to golden oldies. At one time, however, this grand theater hosted such spell-binding movies as *How the West Was Won* and *Born Free.*

Pedaling past First Baptist Church, which our family attended for several years, I crossed Henley Street and proceeded toward the University of Tennessee. I hold a degree from this institution, the Bachelor of Science in Civil Engineering. Marcia and I were dating throughout our academic careers there.

*A Slice of Tennessee*

Many a crisp fall afternoon like this one found us in Neyland Stadium to witness the ecstasy of victory or the agony of defeat, as the Big Orange of Tennessee took on the Alabama Crimson Tide, the Auburn War Eagle, or the Vanderbilt Commodores on the gridiron. Ayres Hall still stands so stately atop The Hill, looking like the epitome of academia.

Just west of the University the Sequoia Hills subdivision with its grand old homes marked the border between older historic Knoxville and the newer commercial development out Kingston Pike. Restaurants, shopping centers, and a variety of stores abounded and showed evidence of constant change. One of the early McDonalds restaurant franchises was established on this stretch of Kingston Pike. Still in operation, it was sporting the huge golden arches of yesteryear. I made a stop at Cedar Bluff Cycles, where they had recently repaired my bike. Tall, pony-tailed Tim assisted me in finding a spare tube for my tire. I showed him a recent article in *The Knoxville Journal* about my trans-state ride. He replied, "Sweet!" He did not charge me for the tube.

**Almost like the original**

*Chapter 4   Knoxville to Kingston*

One observation from big city bike-riding: traffic lights delight in stopping bicycles as frequently as possible, the same as cars. And after stopping at a succession of them, not to mention competing with heavy traffic for pavement space, I was ready to see a little country. The multi-lanes of West Knoxville and Farragut soon yielded to the rural two-lane of Loudon County. Traffic thinned. The road began to serve up delightful landscape. Now I was in unspoiled Tennessee rural countryside! The fall is my favorite season of the year, with its warm days, cool nights, bright colors, and distinctive smells. And rural Tennessee displays all the wonder of the season in grand fashion. Rolling hills, blue skies, shirt-sleeve temperatures, fields with huge hay bales, woods with trees timidly giving up their green in lieu of yellows, reds, and golds—such a day is why people leave less fortunate states to move to Tennessee. I thought I could die of pure pleasure!

Rural countryside soon gives way to small town in this state. After an hour or so of farms and woods, I entered a small built up area centered around an intersection. At the time I did not even know where I was. My brother-in-law Tim recognized the spot as I showed him my pictures later. Most maps do not even designate this crossroads by name. There was not much there but a few businesses and some old-timers' memories. Yet it has a name that radiates southern down-home elegance: Dixie Lee Junction. Even with the Icearium and Little Joe's Pizza flanking the more quaint Court Café, this unincorporated town had the feel of decades long past. Riding through the crossroads, one could sense its former significance: the major intersection of two major highways. Dixie Highway is actually the name for a system of highways (including US 70) which was originally built to connect the Midwest with the southern states. The system designated Lee Highway (including US 11) tied New York City with San Francisco, via the South. And they crossed right here. Rumor has it that the town was named after Bing Crosby's first wife, Dixie Lee, who grew up in nearby Harriman. The less romantic but more likely origin of the name is the highways.

Hence, my discovery of Dixie Lee Junction. Having lived in Knoxville as a teenager, I had heard that name before. I'd even passed through here without knowing where I was. Decades ago at the end of an enjoyable Sunday drive after church, Dad took Mom and us kids to a barbecue restaurant called Otts. I remember the odd name and the strong recommendation of my Dad's coworker. (It *was* good barbecue.) Imagine my surprise at seeing it again after forty years—this time by bicycle.

**Once a major cross roads**

Back out in the rural countryside again the steep upgrade began. Now I realize that hills and valleys are part of a cross-state bike ride. But memories of the endless up-and-downs of the Dandridge to Knoxville stretch began to loom large. This section, however, was up-and-up, top a rise only to see another rise

*Chapter 4    Knoxville to Kingston*

unfold before me.  I began to wonder, would this upgrade never end?  My muscles started aching.  I pedaled by faith, just knowing the next bend would reveal a long, breezy downgrade.  It didn't happen.  I finally did hit some short downhill sections of highway, but I learned a new corollary to Murphy's Law for Bicyclists:  Downgrades never equal upgrades.  My thirst was raging, my legs crying for relief.  I thought I could die of pure fatigue!  Rounding a bend, I happened upon an oasis in the desert:  a little convenience store with cold drinks, shade, and a clerk named Jessie, who allowed some conversation and a bench to sit and rest.  No I-40 rest area ever looked so good.

Kingston, a busy little town centered around the Roane County Courthouse, came into view after a few more upgrades.  While it had traffic, red lights, commerce, and lots of people like the big cities, it nevertheless had the charm and personality of a small town.  I proudly took a picture of the courthouse with my bicycle in front only to discover that there was a second courthouse right next door, a much older one.  A plaque beside it informed the world of the town's claim to fame:  for one whole day Kingston was the capital of Tennessee.  Apparently, in order to satisfy a treaty agreement with the Cherokees, the capital had to be relocated from Knoxville to Kingston.  So the Tennessee General Assembly convened there—for just one day.  Afterward, they resumed meeting in Knoxville.  I couldn't help but wonder how the Cherokees and lobbyists reacted the next day to find the capital missing.

Knoxville, Dixie Lee Junction, Kingston, rural Tennessee—What a city!  What towns!  What a state!  You might even call them *Grand*!

*A Slice of Tennessee*

**The big city (UT's Ayres Hall)**

**The small town (Old Courthouse, Kingston)**

*Chapter 4   Knoxville to Kingston*

**The open road (notice the upgrade)**

*A Slice of Tennessee*

**45.06 miles for the day**

**107.79 miles total**

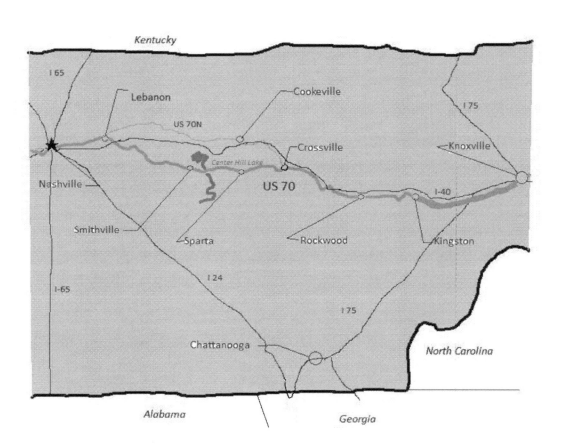

## Chapter 5  Kingston to Crossville
## Downhill to Memphis!

One more major hurdle and the worst would be over. I would soon be biking down easy street. It would be all downhill to Memphis. If not, I didn't want to know. After so many miles of steep grades, my ride for this day would leave me atop the Cumberland Plateau. Not bad for a senior citizen.

I was beginning the fourth leg of my journey across the state, Kingston to Crossville. Quite frankly I was dreading it. The near-constant up and down from Dandridge to Knoxville to Kingston, while exhilarating, had been hard work. And now I faced the daunting Cumberland Plateau. Do the math. The average elevation of Kingston is 764 feet. The average elevation of Crossville is 1890 feet. It's all uphill—a lot. This ride would not be an easy one.

*A Slice of Tennessee*

Yet only a few minutes out on the road, my Diamondback Crestview began to work its magic once more. It had been two weeks since I last rode. Marcia had spent the previous weekend in Nashville visiting her ailing father in the hospital. My weekend was spent in the back yard digging holes for some badly needed shrubbery. But honestly—pedaling US 70 in East Tennessee in the fall beats digging holes any day!

It was partly cloudy and brisk as I started out in Kingston. My Dad tells me I am not the first Horner to make family history in this town. My Uncle Marion (Dad's brother) preceded me there.

In the late 1930's Dad and Marion were young pre-teens growing up in Washington, D.C., where my grandfather (William Isaac Horner) was a lobbyist for the postal workers. My grandmother's mom lived with them. She and Marion did not enjoy the best of relationships.

One afternoon, after a particularly harsh scolding, Marion accidently knocked Great-grandma's eyeglasses off her face as he tried to brush past her. She thought he did it on purpose, and Marion decided the prudent thing to do was to leave—fast. So he and a close friend set out hitchhiking. Their frantic families had no word of them for a full week. Finally, they received a long distance call from the police in Kingston, who had found them thumbing a ride on US 70 and picked them up. My grandfather asked the police to hold them until he could get there a couple of days later. And hold them they did—in the county jail. Apparently Marion and his buddy were trying to reach Waverly, Tennessee, home of Uncle Jesse. They nearly succeeded.

I pedaled again past the Roane County Courthouse in Kingston. This courthouse was recently the scene of a more ominous incident. On August 9, 2005, felon George Hyatte was in court on a charge of armed robbery. Handcuffed and shackled at the feet, he and several other prisoners were about to be transported by police van back to Brushy Mountain State Prison, where he

*Chapter 5  Kingston to Crossville*

was already serving a sentence for robbery and assault.  Suddenly, a Ford Explorer pulled up behind the group, and George's wife Jennifer jumped out, armed with a handgun.  In response to her husband's shouts of "Shoot him!", she fired repeatedly, hitting officer Wayne "Cotton" Morgan in the abdomen and fatally wounding him.  As another officer returned fire, George jumped into the SUV, and the two sped away.  Less than two days later, authorities captured them at a hotel in Columbus, Ohio.  Jennifer had received serious wounds in the gun battle at the courthouse.  The Hyattes each have subsequently received life sentences without the possibility of parole.  The press referred to the couple as a modern-day Bonnie and Clyde.

A sad footnote to the above tragic story is that the night before this violent crime, county commissioners had just voted to build a new justice center with an inside "sally port" security area for loading and unloading prisoners.

It was difficult to imagine such violence as I drank in the charm of Kingston on my way out of town.  The bridge leading out of the city over the Clinch River was a fairly new, attractive-looking reinforced concrete structure.  Pedaling across it this fall day, I experienced again that sensation of being suspended in mid-air.  If only my camera were working properly.  The zoom feature was broken, it didn't focus well, and now, even the stick was full.  I'd miss some good pictures that day.

It was a typical run-of-the-mill breath-takingly beautiful fall day in Tennessee—temperatures brisk but not cold, the sun bright but muted enough to allow maximum enjoyment of the colors.  The trees were not yet at peak, but occasional orange and gold blazes appeared among the green.  It was warm pedaling uphill, chilly coasting downhill, and deliciously cool on the level.  My bright orange University of Tennessee sweatshirt was appropriate attire.  Good football weather.

**Biking a bridge is better than driving it any day**

Rockwood was blessedly flat. It is the last town of any size before ascending the dreaded mountain to the plateau. How many times had I been through Rockwood as a child, a teenager, a college student while traversing I-40 between Knoxville and Nashville? High above the town, the interstate highway snakes along the mountain ridge with panoramic views of the valley and town below. But for many years this section of highway remained the last unfinished link of I-40 in Tennessee. Construction had been plagued with rock slides. So traffic detoured through Rockwood.

Finally in the mid-1970's the road was completed and the town bypassed. Many times afterward, I would view Rockwood from the highway above. Now I was looking up trying to trace out the interstate from Rockwood below.

During the years of detour, Rockwood's traffic lights regularly frustrated motorists with frequent stops. The lights were still up. They seemed to delight in stopping bicycles, too. Traffic lights in big cities stop traffic as often as

*Chapter 5  Kingston to Crossville*

possible out of pure meanness.  In small towns they do it out of a sense of civic duty.  The net result is the same.  But I am not Lance Armstrong.  I am not in a hurry.

Out of Rockwood the dreaded uphill stretch took on its own character.  Yet, except for occasional stops for breath and Gatorade, I was hardly conscious of the steep upgrade.  There were long stretches of quiet, broken only by sounds from the woods, the rustle of the leaves, water from a far-off creek, and only occasionally, a car.  On some sections of roadway, the scene was so idyllic that one would swear that the highway formed naturally at the prompting of God, like some of the nearby sandstone rock cliffs.

*Ozone*.  The name sounds like an environmental concern.  The original name of this stop in the road was *Mammy* (after a local creek—honest to goodness, there is a *Pappy Creek* also).  But when a post office was located here in 1896, apparently the locals desired a more sophisticated name.  Hence, the name Ozone, for the clean, fresh smell of the air after a thunderstorm.

One of the best-kept secrets in Tennessee is the waterfall of the same name located on Fall Creek.  Dad pointed it out to me on a trip through here in the sixties.  The waterfall is barely a quarter mile off the highway.  Indeed, during the winter months motorists can see the falls from the highway through the bare trees.

Fall Creek Falls in Middle Tennessee is also located on a Fall Creek.  The two waterfalls look remarkably similar.  Both consist of a sheer drop from a high cliff (110 feet for Ozone Falls vs. 256 feet for Fall Creek Falls) with the water hitting the rocks below like a bathroom shower and cascading from there into a bowl-shaped pool at the bottom.

Most Tennesseans are familiar with Fall Creek Falls, but few are even aware of the existence of Ozone Falls.  Viewed from the top or from the pool at the bottom in a deep gorge, this natural wonder was worth pedaling up the mountain to see. On this particular day the water had slowed to a trickle due to dry weather conditions. But rain was in the forecast.

**Ozone Falls: another of Tennessee's well-kept secrets**

Is predicting the weather an art or a science? Benjamin Franklin once said, "Some folks are weather-wise; most are otherwise." But apparently ole Ben never knew the late Helen Lane of Crab Orchard. Did I really pass through Crab Orchard? I saw the sign for it but nothing that looked like a town. Of course, I was busy keeping a sharp eye out for wooly worms as I pedaled through this community. According to Mrs. Lane, wooly worms are a strong indicator of the coming winter. If the critters are brown, it portends a mild winter; if black, a harsh one. Black with a brown ring in the middle signifies a harsh winter with a brief mild spell in January.

As a boy growing up in Knoxville, I marveled at this lady's ability to do with squirrel firs, hornet nests, and other signs of nature what trained

*Chapter 5  Kingston to Crossville*

meteorologists needed satellites to do.  An elderly deacon in my church in Campbell County predicted winter weather by examining sunflower seeds.  He would have loved to compare notes with Mrs. Lane.

A clerk at Rowell's Apple House and Motel near Crossville informed me that Mrs. Lane had passed away about five years previously.  Her daughter continues the weather-predicting.  The clerk couldn't remember the daughter's name but said she married a Hedgecoth.  I was pleased to hear that someone is continuing the tradition.

Pedaling into Crossville, I was exhilarated with the satisfaction of another forty miles or so behind me.  I'd seen a number of interesting sights.  If only my camera weren't acting up.  I would have only nine pictures to show for such a day and some of them too fuzzy to use.  We simply *had* to get a new camera.  True to its name, Crossville is a crossroads of seven major highways.  Even US 70 splits here into 70 and 70N.  Established around 1800 as *Lambeth Crossroads*, the town took on the moniker *Crossville* about thirty years later when it received its first post office.

I wasn't ready to stop quite yet; so I continued on about seven miles down US 70N toward Cookeville.  Notice I said *down*.  Marcia had looked at furniture in Crossville and bought some mums for the house at a nursery. She quickly appeared to pick me up at the University of Tennessee's Experiment Station Road.

Where to next—Cookeville?  Carthage?  The logistics would be a challenge.  It was too far now to ride and come back home at night.  But I had scaled the mountain, ascended the plateau.  My dread was unfounded, for the ride had not been difficult at all.  So the worst was behind me.  The *worst*?  But I had enjoyed every minute of this ride.  And now it was all downhill to Memphis!

*A Slice of Tennessee*

**Downhill as far as the eye can see!**

***44.90 miles for the day***

***152.69 miles total***

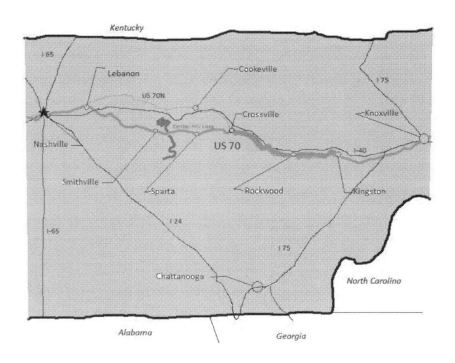

# Chapter 6  Crossville to Smithville
## Serendipities

The northern route just made more sense. It was shorter, flatter, and looked far more interesting. Good accommodations for food and lodging were more readily available. And the southern route looked bland by comparison. How could such towns as Smithville and Liberty possibly compete with the major university and railroad museum of Cookeville? Liberty's claim to fame is—honest to goodness—the caricature of a mule painted on a local bluff by a local resident. Besides, I had already ridden seven miles down the northern route west of Crossville on my previous ride. Yes, the northern route was the logical choice. So I chose the southern route.

Finally, I was on my way again! I was not stuck in Crossville anymore. It was mid-November now, nearly a month since my last ride. The weather was clear and cold (28 degrees with a predicted high of 47)—there would not be many more good riding days before winter set in. I was eager to get pedaling

*A Slice of Tennessee*

again.  But which route to take?  Just west of Crossville, US 70 splits into US 70N, which follows a northern path through Cookeville and Carthage, and US 70, which winds a southern path through Sparta, Smithville, and sundry other small towns.  All along I had planned to ride US 70N.  At the last minute, on a lark, I opted for the southern route.  After all, I had never been to Sparta or Smithville that I could recall.  Besides, this route crosses the Caney Fork River/Center Hill Lake, and bridges spanning broad bodies of water are always fun to bike across.  At any rate, I would see some Tennessee I had not seen before.  I was game.  And I was in for some surprises.

This ride was different from previous ones.  I was on my own; Marcia could not come along in the chase car this time. That prospect was a little scary—if I broke a spoke, had leg cramps or some other mishap, there would be no one to bail me out.  And riding this far west now complicated the logistics. This trip required creative planning to get dropped off and picked up at the right place at the right time.  The ride would span three days.  That meant two nights' lodging.  A thorough internet search finally turned up a mom-and-pop motel on Center Hill Lake near Smithville.  (I just hoped they had clean sheets.)  For the second night, near Lebanon, a departure of a few miles from the main route would net a reliable but affordable chain hotel.

A rental vehicle solved the problem of getting to my starting point. Enterprise has offices in both LaFollette and Crossville.  A two-hour drive quite early brought me within two miles of downtown Crossville.  The bike easily fit in the back of the vehicle.  The change from the Eastern to the Central time zone worked in my favor, so I could still get an early start.  The clerks at Enterprise were quite friendly and helpful—they didn't even blink when I told them I was about to ride that bike to Smithville.  If they thought I was crazy to set out in such cold weather, they didn't let on.   Indeed, the whole day had the feel of a "Go!"  A good start would be the first of many serendipities on this trip.

*Chapter 6   Crossville to Smithville*

**ser-en-dip-i-ty**--*noun*: the faculty or phenomenon of finding valuable or agreeable things not sought for ; *also* : an instance of this.[1]

The term *serendipity* was coined by Horace Walpole of England in 1754 after a Persian fairy tale entitled *The Three Princes of Serendip*.  In the tale three men on an adventurous road trip make many seemingly irrelevant discoveries which prove in the end to be quite fortuitous.   In layman's terms a serendipity is something real good you weren't looking for.

The road to Sparta reminded me that there are still Tennesseans who are not ashamed of their Christian faith and values.  One billboard loudly proclaimed, "Jesus said, 'Ye must be born again.'"  A little further along a lighthouse and large sign marked the home of Jesus Never Fails Church.  A few more miles revealed The Way Café and Pizzeria (its sign shaped like a cross).  The tiny stop-in-the-road town of Pomona boasted no less than four churches (two Baptist, one Methodist, and one Full Gospel).  Of course this was the Bible Belt, but I don't always see enough evidence of the faith anymore, even here.  A nice little *serendipity*.

Bad surprises can come along, too.  Guess what?  It's **not** all downhill to Memphis from Crossville!  There were plenty of hills that morning and a raw headwind to boot.  Blue jeans, a sweat shirt, a jacket, and ear coverings helped to shut out the chill morning air, but they also added to the weight I had to pull up those upgrades that weren't supposed to be there.  A backpack rounded out my attire.  I had packed as light as possible for a three-day trip; nevertheless, it was surprising how heavy a little underwear could be.

---

[1] Merriam-Webster online dictionary

*A Slice of Tennessee*

But how could I despair?  Middle Tennessee hills are milder than their East Tennessee counterparts.  Besides, the day had turned out beautiful—clear skies of deep blue, a waning half-moon setting over the western horizon, trees reluctant to let go of their colors.  And I was finally on my way again, no longer stuck in Crossville.  I was on my bicycle and going somewhere despite major logistical problems, with a new camera the Lord had provided just days earlier.  *Serendipities* all.

It occurred to me that I hadn't had much meaningful contact with local people as yet on my ride across the state, perhaps because previous trips had lasted less than a day with Marcia immediately picking me up.  Or perhaps I was just in too much of a hurry, despite my boasts otherwise.  Or perhaps after daily personal interactions with others in my pastoral role, my more or less introverted nature just enjoyed long stretches of solitude surrounded by Tennessee.  Whatever the reason, I determined to meet more people this trip.

Gliding through the unincorporated town of Pleasant Hill, I was reminded of my pastorate at a church of the same name.  I began my fulltime ministry there twenty-one years earlier.  It was a rural congregation outside of a town named Orlinda.  Most of the men of the church were tobacco farmers (a traditional Tennessee cash crop).  One such farmer named Jeff suddenly got on fire for the Lord and would take me around to visit all his lost or backslidden buddies.  He even took me once to visit Other (pronounced OH-thur) and his son David.  "They make home brew," he explained, "and I used to buy from them sometimes before the Lord convicted me about drinking."  When we arrived, I noticed a huge pile of chopped wood in their back yard, more than seemed necessary to heat the house till spring.  I didn't ask any questions nor did I call the revenuers on them—we just talked to them about the Lord.  Jeff

*Chapter 6    Crossville to Smithville*

was a motorcycle rider with a love for the road similar to mine. He would ride Tennessee rural highways, then come home and use a yellow highlighter to mark the roads he'd been down, even as I was currently highlighting US 70 on my own map, piece by piece.

I was now entering White County. Revolutionary soldier and surveyor John White was the first known white settler in this region, having moved his family here in 1789. Although a state historical marker claims (and most locals agree) that the county is named for this White, some historians hold that it was originally named for Revolutionary War General James White of Knoxville.

My leg muscles were beginning to hurt. Even these mild hills were working a number on them. I was about three miles away from Sparta and a good lunch—surely I could hold out that long. But out of nowhere a long, steep downgrade suddenly appeared—with no corresponding upgrade. I was finally coming off the plateau! I had earned this easy, breezy section many times over, but I did not expect it so soon. Half way down this hill and around a bend came another surprise: a scenic overlook, beckoning me to stop and rest and enjoy the vista of hills and valleys. How soothing to both the eyes and legs—now this was a real *serendipity*. There was even a bench to sit on and prolong the process of recharging. I hated to leave this oasis, but at least Sparta was just a couple of miles away now.

Moments later, near the bottom of the downgrade, a sign lured me off the highway yet again, this time down a side road to see the "Historic Rock House." I had no idea what this house was or why it was historic. But wasn't I wanting to slow down and enjoy the ride? Wasn't I wanting to meet more people? Here was an unexpected opportunity.

The Rock House was a one-room, 187-year-old building constructed of the ubiquitous local sandstone of this county. The house was all original except for a small living area added to the back for the caretakers. According to the historic marker out front, the structure was used as a toll house and stagecoach inn for decades in the 1800's. Bill Austin was busy trimming the shrubbery around the house. He stopped to invite me inside for the grand tour. "Andrew Jackson, James K. Polk, Sam Houston, and Sequoia have spent nights within these same walls," he explained with the quiet excitement of one who truly appreciated Tennessee history. "When you rode the stagecoach over this road, it took a full eighteen hours to make the thirteen miles from Pleasant Hill. The ride from Knoxville to Nashville took a full week. They would usually stop here for a night's rest, and you might find yourself in the company of a president or a congressman."

**Andrew Jackson really did sleep here!**

Bill's mother Girda joined us as we continued the one-room tour. They showed me numerous relics as they related the colorful history of this rest stop and were particularly proud of a porcelain teapot decorating a shelf. "Daniel Boone's niece Sarah once owned that teapot," Bill explained. "Her father was

*Chapter 6   Crossville to Smithville*

scalped and killed in an Indian attack on their pilgrimage west." Apparently those were perilous times. In fact, highwaymen were a significant threat to any party traveling that road. In order to protect their overnight guests, hosts of the Rock House would not only stand guard; they would also hide their guests in the attic, with only a small, covered ceiling opening as access. Even if the highwaymen could overpower the guard and find the ceiling panel, it is doubtful they could effectively enter the opening and attack the then-aroused passengers.

Bill told me proudly that the Rock House is the second building bought by the state—in 1947—for historic preservation. (I have yet to learn the first.) Chewing gum magnate William Wrigley once owned some ground near here at the top of the mountain. That explains the "Spearmint Lane" I had passed earlier in the day. Before I mounted my bike again, I asked Bill and Girda for guidance on where to eat lunch in Sparta. After some debate between them, Girda recommended a few good restaurants. This stop was certainly a delight I was not anticipating—a *serendipity*!

**Bill and Girda are proud of that teapot**

*A Slice of Tennessee*

Sparta is a quaint town with friendly people and obvious civic pride.  It is a clean-looking city, a little larger than I expected.  Tastefully designed sidewalks, benches, and street lights add to the city's charm.  The Calfkiller River, which bisects it, begged me to pause and snap a picture.  This scenic stream is much more docile than its violent name.  (Actually, it was named for a Cherokee Indian chief who once lived in the area.)  Sparta is the only town of any size located on this river, which winds its way down toward Van Buren County and eventually joins the Caney Fork River.

Sparta is also the home of the late Lester Raymond Flatt.  Singer-guitarist Flatt and his banjo-picking buddy Earl Scruggs, both formerly of Bill Monroe's Bluegrass Boys band, joined forces in 1948 and with their Foggy Mountain Boys helped set the tone for bluegrass music until their parting in 1969.  Their "Ballad of Jed Clampett" was used as the theme song for the hit television show *The Beverly Hillbillies*.  Flatt (posthumously) and Scruggs were inducted into the Country Music Hall of Fame in 1985.  Lester Flatt Memorial Bluegrass Day is observed annually in Sparta as part of their Liberty Square Celebration.  A granite monument to Flatt sits in the center of town.

Lunch took place at the 2nd Act Deli (Girda's first choice) on Mayberry Street.  I had to stop and ask directions, something no man should ever have to admit.  But I was hungry.  Two young laborers in the heart of town, both wearing distinctive prison stripes, listened courteously but did not know where the street was.  I next stopped in at an investment office where three well-dressed men were in discussion.  They were only too glad to point me toward my street.  One block further two dogs ran out at the bicyclist.  One was all bark but no bite.  The other was too lazy even to bark.

*Chapter 6   Crossville to Smithville*

2nd Act did not really seem to be a deli so much as a diner.  And the name seemed to imply to me a Broadway play motif.  Yet all the décor suggested Hollywood: empty film canisters on tables and posters on the walls of such movies as *The Postman Always Rings Twice* and *East of Eden.*  In between the posters were pictures of Audrey Hepburn, Paul Newman, James Dean, and of course, Lester Flatt.  The walls were quite entertaining.  And regardless of the meaning of the name, this place served a swell hamburger, grilled over charcoal.  The French fries were real too.   I certainly was not disappointed.  And the owner even came around to make sure I was enjoying my serendipitous meal.

**Their hamburgers were great**

Starting back out toward the highway, I saw the white on green guide sign indicating Smithville, and suddenly I was eager to pedal down the open road again.  With a happy stomach, a now-sunny day, and more Tennessee to discover by bike, I felt blessed.

*A Slice of Tennessee*

Nice wide paved shoulders are ideal for biking down a busy highway, and this road had them. Unfortunately, a short ways out of town the shoulders narrowed and turned into rough gravel and tar, not a comfortable riding surface. I rode in the travel lane as much as possible, pulling onto the rough shoulder only when necessary. My little helmet rear-view mirror has paid for itself many times over. As larger vehicles roared past me, it occurred to me again how blessed I was—I had the privilege of riding this road at bike speed in the open air; these drivers had to traverse it in motorized vehicles.

And it's funny the little things you notice at bike speed that you might miss in a car or truck. For instance. Kudzu takes on a whole different persona as it dies and turns brown for the winter. And did you know there is a Will-Mar convenience store along this highway—could it be that Marcia and I have a sideline? Also, as I passed "Barbie Farm," I couldn't help but scratch my head—I thought they made those dolls in factories.

Passing by a rock quarry, I caught my first glimpse of the bedrock limestone that underlies so much of Middle Tennessee. Not much further, the road carried me through a limestone cut on a roughly 2:1 slope. That dated this section of roadway. Since the early 1970's such rock cut sections have been presplit with nearly vertical walls. As a college cooperative engineering program student, studying half the year and working half the year, I learned about this process from my employer, McDowell-Purcell, Inc. They specialized in site preparation work and had actually perfected the presplitting process.

My muscles were getting weary again but thankfully no leg cramps. Around 3:00 pm, I finally came upon Caney Fork River/Center Hill Lake. There was a long steep downgrade leading to the bridge over this body of water. I groaned inside, knowing there would surely be a corresponding steep upgrade

*Chapter 6  Crossville to Smithville*

on the other side.  Nevertheless I started down this hill with anticipation.  I had been looking forward to this crossing.  The river/lake is a pretty one, and again, I enjoy pedaling long spans high up over water.  Now if you're expecting it, it's not really a serendipity.  But I was surprised again.  This crossing was an old two lane steel truss bridge, only the second one I've encountered on my ride so far. With my engineering background old bridges fascinate me. In a stately fashion they bear quiet witness to an era rapidly slipping away, when all long road trips took place over highways like this one, with fresh slices of Americana around every bend.  When I was a young boy, our grandmother took my sister Joyce and me on one such trip from Jacksonville, Florida, to Waverly, Tennessee, traveling mostly over roads just like this one.  To keep us amused, she bought us a card game in which the players looked for objects along the roadside to match their cards (hamburger stand, cemetery, railroad crossing, courthouse, etc.).  I now wondered, what do such games (I'm sure they still sell them) put on the cards today—exit signs? D.O.T. workers mowing the median? construction zones?  Again, I felt blessed.

The lake was breath-taking.  Center Hill Lake is one of the cleanest man-made lakes in Tennessee.  With the afternoon sun cutting across it, the waters were shimmering. Had it really been thirty-four years since my college pal Phil Mabry had brought Barry Chamberlain and me up to this lake to water ski?  On that trip we had not made it as far as Smithville.  I was looking forward to seeing the town.

The trip across the bridge was worth a whole day's pedaling.  But now it was time to pay the piper: the steep upgrade.  I began slowly, took my time. There was no need to hurry.  By the yard it's hard; by the inch it's a cinch (well, sort of).  Only six more miles remained to Smithville and the mom and pop motel I was searching for.  Actually it was more like five miles, but I was trying to fool my mind so my destination would appear sooner than expected. (Such tricks rarely work). I'd likely arrive within thirty to forty-five minutes.

But no sooner had I crested the hill on the other side of the bridge than the Center Hill Inn came into view, farther out from town than I had thought. My ride was over for the day! I didn't even have to play tricks on my mind. And this place looked great! It was small, only twelve units, each of which overlooked the lake below with a fantastic view. I didn't see a lot of cars around, so surely there was a vacancy. Parking my bike, I entered with an explanation all ready as to why I could not supply a car make and model and tag number on the registration card.

**What a view for $50 a night!**

Nicole the desk clerk was a pleasant lady. Yes, they had a room available; I could park my bike inside. And, she added, I arrived just in time.

*Chapter 6   Crossville to Smithville*

She and the other employees were about to close up and leave for the day. I would be the *only* guest (indeed the only human being) that night at this establishment, which did indeed have clean sheets and quite comfortable rooms. Suddenly a thought occurred to me: "Does that mean your restaurant also is closed for tonight?" It did indeed. I started the mental calculations—five miles into town, five miles back out. The last time I checked that was still a total of ten. "How far are we from the nearest convenience store," I asked, now trying desperately to save my weary muscles the extra mileage, even at the cost of a stale sandwich for supper. Nicole and her friend discussed the question and finally settled on three to four miles (actually it was almost five). "But," she quickly added, "I don't mind at all staying long enough to fix you whatever you want off our restaurant menu, and you can take it back to your room for later." Her friend quickly added, "I live right across the road. I've got some soft drinks in my refrigerator if you want any." Reprieved!

Of course I was hoping for a good end to this delightful day of riding, but I never expected such a nice room at such a reasonable price with such privacy and such service (a good dinner, too). A wonderful day, a wonderful stay. **Serendipity!**

*A Slice of Tennessee*

**Steel truss bridges fascinate me**

*Chapter 6   Crossville to Smithville*

**47.69 miles for the day**

**200.38 miles total**

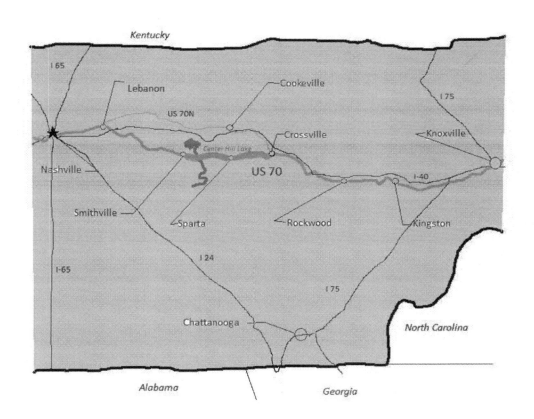

*A Slice of Tennessee*

# Chapter 7  Smithville to Lebanon
## A Character Counts

"A City for the Children, A Character Counts"—so reads the message on a billboard along US 70 welcoming the traveler into Lebanon. And it seemed to be the perfect theme for my ride that day from Smithville.

Thursday dawned clear and cold, 35 degrees on its way up to 49 for the high. There was a gusty wind (in the wrong direction, of course). But it was a good day for biking. I'd had a good night's rest at a great motel and was itching to get underway. What a thrill to wake up knowing I would fill my day with two things I enjoy so much: bike riding and Tennessee. I was out of my room even before the clerks arrived for the day.

This trip was a blessing from God. Its proximity to Thanksgiving (a week away) only added to my sense of gratitude for my health, the bicycle, the opportunity, and Tennessee (not necessarily in that order).

*A Slice of Tennessee*

I believe that every child has an inherent God-given sense of wonder that dims and fades over time as adult responsibilities increase and life's hard knocks multiply. That sense of wonder explains a child's fascination with an autumn leaf or excitement over a sled ride.

Marcia and I took a badly needed vacation many years ago when our children, Joshua and Susanna, were quite young. As Joshua, age five, stood looking out at the Gulf of Mexico for the very first time, his hand in mine, his sense of wonder at the immensity of the scene before him spilled out into words. "How did they make it, Dad? Did they just dig a big hole or what?" I had the immense privilege of telling him that men could not make the natural phenomenon in front of him—God Himself made it. Susanna, for her part at age three, looked around with wide eyes every time we entered our little white Chevette. "Where are we going now?" The very concept of a trip away from home filled her with wonder.

On occasion God allows us adults to recapture something of that sense of awe. Biking under this sunny but cold blue autumn sky (headwind notwithstanding) kindled afresh a child-like fascination with the world around me. I was starting out here near Smithville and going—somewhere.

"Character" refers to features that are distinctive or interesting. That term can apply to much of what I'd seen so far on my bike ride across our interesting and distinctive state. But it would seem especially appropriate on this leg of the journey. Nothing flashy, nothing spectacular—but many sights worth seeing that add up to a slice of Tennessee, with character.

After checking myself out of the Center Hill Inn, I pedaled into Smithville looking for a light and quick breakfast. Passing Me-Ma's Restaurant, its window proudly proclaiming its #1 Breakfast, I was tempted to stop. But, no, with miles to go before I next slept, I wanted to be on my way, with a light load in my stomach. Passing Hardees, I almost stopped again, thinking a quick sausage biscuit might fill the bill. But Hardees was on the opposite side of the busy

*Chapter 7   Smithville to Lebanon*

highway.  Besides, was I biking across Tennessee just to dine in an omnipresent fast food chain?  No, I wisely overcame all resistance and stopped at Susie's Restaurant for a sit-down breakfast of eggs, biscuits with gravy, sausage, hash browns, and orange juice—a breakfast with character.  Susie's itself was full of characters that morning, white-haired men's clubs dawdling over their coffee and solving the world's problems, apparently a daily ritual.

The world always looks better after a big, hot breakfast.  Smithville was a little larger than I expected.  Not being a county seat, it has no square—just a long stretch of four-lane.  It reminded me of a town I once saw in Maryland called Mt. Vernon.  A local waterman declared it to be "the longest city on the Eastern Shore:  nine miles long and two houses deep."  I had possibly seen Smithville before in 1974.  College buddy Phil Mabry's family had a small home on nearby Center Hill Lake.  Phil had taken Barry Chamberlain and me water skiing.  I remember how clear and cool the water was every time I wiped out.  As I pedaled on out of the city, numerous storage facilities for boats offered mute testimony to the continuing popularity of the lake and its water sports.

Basking in the afterglow of that breakfast, I pedaled on down the broad five-lane section of US 70.  Why would the Tennessee D.O.T. put a two-way-left-turn-lane in a rural area with no driveways to turn left into?  My supervisor in the Traffic Engineering Division of T.D.O.T many years earlier told me that such a lane in such an area helps to separate oncoming vehicles and significantly cuts down on head-on collisions.  Reason enough.

Other mundane yet interesting mini-slices of Tennessee continued to pass by.  I crossed over Dry Creek.  It was.  Ever hear of Toad Road?  (Perhaps somewhere there is a Bullfrog Boulevard.)  Rock outcroppings seemed to win out over arable soil for surface area on one farm I passed.  A stone chimney standing alone amid the rocks testified to the hard labors of the family that once eked out a living from that land.  I could only imagine trying to grow crops and raise livestock on such ground.  Further down on the opposite side was the

59

defunct "Country Bar & Grill," boarded up and losing a battle with weeds. You see a lot of long-gone businesses along older secondary highways.

**At least it rhymes!**

Limestone outcroppings and rock cuts through hills were becoming more frequent now. Here and there cedar trees grew contentedly right out of the most inhospitable stretches of rock. Those cedars will grow almost anywhere. Cedars of Lebanon State Park nearby plays host to scads of the trees and therefore bears a striking resemblance to the middle-eastern country. Chunks of local limestone—stacked with care and precision, often by slave labor—formed ancient fences lining many sections of the highway.

Ever hear of the town of Shop Springs? You're not alone. How about Cherry Valley? I hadn't either. But the character of the locals was on display via a bumper sticker on the unincorporated town's official sign: "Liberals: French for *cowards*."

On I pedaled, looking forward to Liberty. Now there was a town with character. Founded in 1797 by Adam Dale, a Revolutionary war veteran, this

*Chapter 7    Smithville to Lebanon*

community likely was named in honor of liberty from Great Britain. The town boasts 367 residents and is accessed via the old two-lane highway, which departs for a mile or two from the main road in order to shield the shy town from view. Indeed, without the school and a convenience store, through traffic on US 70 might pass Liberty unawares.

Although I was tempted to pedal down the two-lane to see the town proper, I stayed on the main, multi-lane highway to avoid missing Liberty's one claim to fame:  the caricature of a mule painted on a limestone bluff next to the highway. What, I wondered, could make a little bluff graffiti so popular with the locals? When the state widened the highway in 2003, local citizens were fearful that the new construction would destroy their local masterpiece. They began a letter-writing campaign and placed signs along the road saying, "Save the Mule." The State of Tennessee maintains that the mule was never in danger of removal. Perhaps, but the rock cliff on which she is painted is part of one small section of bluff that survived the surgical construction that widened the road.

For decades no one knew who had painted the old girl in the first place. Some thought perhaps it was Lavader Woodard, a local photographer whose name is painted on the bluff. But historian Thomas G. Webb cleared up the mystery upon finding a 1957 article in *The Smithville Review* by Dr. Wayne T. Robinson of Dallas. As a 21-year-old college student and resident of Liberty in 1906, Dr. Robinson had climbed the bluff on a lark and painted the mule with coal tar. His creation was patterned after Maud the Mule of a popular comic strip of that day.

*And Her Name Was Maud* was the creation of cartoonist Frederick Burr Opper. The Hearst newspapers hired him in 1899 to draw comic strips. In addition to *Maud*, Opper also produced *Happy Hooligan* and *Alphonse and Gaston*. Maud made her debut in 1904. She was an ornery creature who liked to kick people, especially her owner Si Slocum. In one memorable strip Slocum was so fed up with Maud that he tied her reins to a stake on a motorized race track (yes, they did race cars even back then) hoping for the worst. It didn't turn out as planned. As one racecar after another roared toward her, she'd turn and kick it to smithereens. When Si returned to learn her fate, she kicked him off his feet, glared at him in triumph, and pronounced a hearty "Hee Haw!"

I had no idea where to look for Maud. However, local residents were only too glad to direct me to the site. Naturally, I was expecting this limestone mural to be as large as Mt. Rushmore, or at least as big as a Mack eighteen-wheeler. But it was only about *six feet* across. I almost missed it. I was not disappointed, though. It was worth seeing just for the story behind it. The people take prodigious care of their mule. They have repainted it on several occasions, being careful to preserve the character of the original. A whole town guarding and maintaining a piece of bluff graffiti? Now *that's* character.

**The Tennessee DOT wouldn't touch this masterpiece**

From Liberty I pedaled on down toward Watertown. The road narrows to two lanes somewhere along the way and bypasses the town proper

*Chapter 7   Smithville to Lebanon*

completely. A town with character, however, will not let the traffic just pass it by. A large sign proudly proclaims, "Historic Watertown—Next 4 Exits," as if US 70 were a major, controlled-access, multi-lane freeway. (The "Exits" are short side streets.) The town lives up to its billboard, with its picturesque collection of specialty shops and restaurants on a square centered around a gazebo with piped-in easy-listening music. I stopped in at the local library hoping they were far enough into the twenty-first century to have computers where I could check my email. A gracious librarian regretted to tell me that, while they do have computers and I would certainly be welcome to use one, they were having trouble connecting to the internet that day. This small library was so modern it even had state-of-the-art technological problems.

**Small, but proud of their heritage**

So just what made "Historic Watertown" historic? It was established in 1799 on land given to Colonel Archibald Lytle and his brother William for doing

*A Slice of Tennessee*

their part in the war for our nation's independence. The founder of the town itself, Wilson L. Waters, ran a store and post office and later expanded his enterprises to include a saw mill, a grist mill, and a blacksmith shop. In 1885 the Nashville and Knoxville Railroad built a depot here which brought more business and growth. Songwriter Tom T. Hall released a song in 1997 entitled "Watertown, Tennessee." Garth Brooks filmed a Dr. Pepper commercial on the town square in 2001. And in 2003 the town bucked the national trend of drive-in theaters closing down by opening one of their own: the Stardust Drive-In Theater. These and other notable tidbits of Americana do indeed qualify Watertown for the title "Historic."

Lunch this day would be limited to a Gatorade purchased at a large supermarket and consumed while admiring the beauty of this quaint town. I had had a big breakfast, and I was saving stomach capacity for dinner in Lebanon with a new acquaintance from that area. The afternoon would do its part to develop my appetite, for the highway quickly narrowed, lost almost all shoulder, and became quite hilly. Traffic was heavy, too. I-40 being some distance away, it did not siphon many vehicles off of US 70 along this section.

Finally, I entered Lebanon itself, with its character-proclaiming welcome sign, and I was not disappointed. Signs of character abounded in this delightful city. Just inside the city limits I passed Hellum Funeral Home. The name sounded uncomfortably warm for such a business. Further on I spied an old H. G. Hill food store. I sacked groceries and cleaned the back room at a Hill's food store in Donelson during my high school years. At one time Horace Greeley Hill had quite a chain of stores around Middle Tennessee. Not many remain. He always insisted on closing his stores on Sunday and resisted selling beer, policies overturned only in recent years.

Where was the courthouse square? Apparently US 70 would not intersect it. But I couldn't pass through this city without visiting the square.

*Chapter 7   Smithville to Lebanon*

While I was pondering this dilemma, the offices of *The Lebanon Democrat* newspaper came into view. I wondered if Colleen Campbell Taylor worked there. She had some kind of ties with the news media in the county. I would be meeting with her and her Baptist pastor husband Jonas in a few hours for dinner. So I parked my bike and went inside.

No, the friendly receptionist informed me, no Colleen Taylor worked there. Feeling a need to explain my pungent, sweat-shirted, grubby, backpack-laden persona, I showed her an article from *The Knoxville Journal* about my trans-Tennessee ride. A bicycle-riding preacher? Pedaling across the state? And a senior citizen at that! "Do you mind waiting here for a few minutes? I think J.R. would want to know about this."

Moments later a tall, thin, thirty-ish reporter with dark hair and a big smile appeared out of nowhere bearing my article in one hand while extending the other. "I'm J.R. Lind," he informed, as he deftly ushered me into a side conference room. From somewhere he produced a yellow legal pad. "Get Bill in here with his camera," he shouted to the receptionist excitedly.

Immediately he began to pepper me with questions. Where and when did I start? How long would I ride that day? When did I expect to reach Memphis? And the big one, Why was I doing this crazy ride in cold weather at my age? The whole time we talked Bill Cook was busy snapping pictures.

This interview was delightful! After miles of lonely pedaling it was nice to have a little attention. On an earlier ride I had stopped in at a newspaper office in another town to see if they'd be interested in a story on my ride. I think the receptionist there had me confused with the invisible man. Barely looking up, she explained quickly that they had deadlines and no one was free to talk with me at that time. I understood and later sent an email with my story to one of the reporters, but apparently he was not much interested. But here in Lebanon, where character counts, I suddenly had the feeling that I'd handed J.R. and *The Lebanon Democrat* a gift. And it was a *nice* feeling!

As the interview concluded, Bill asked if they could get some photos with my bicycle outside. A US 70 highway marker just outside the front door afforded an excellent backdrop. Then, interview over, J.R. and I stood talking for a few minutes in front of the ancient Line-O-Type printing press which graces the entrance to the building. He told me about his love for journalism. He was responsible for reporting on everything from sports to courts, business to family and faith. His article on me would prove to be a winner: "Meet the Peddlin' Preacher from LaFollette."

With some directions from J.R., I finally managed to find the courthouse square. But this square had something most do not: a log cabin off to one side with a still-flowing spring nearby. This cabin belonged to Neddie Jacobs, the first settler to build a cabin near this water source. He built it in a grove of red cedars. These cedars inspired commissioners for the new town to name the place *Lebanon* after the biblical land of cedars. The spring, called Big Spring, served the community for over a hundred years until 1908.

**Don't think anyone lives there anymore**

*Chapter 7   Smithville to Lebanon*

The square had a further claim on my interest that day. J.R. informed me that Sam Houston, the Tennessee-Texas hero of Andrew Jackson's day had once practiced law in an office near the square. I was amazed at the number of individuals I asked for the exact location of the plaque commemorating such a historic personage who could not tell me where it was though they pass by it every day. Finally a clerk at a local bank was able to point me toward it. Indeed, Sam Houston's office had stood on that spot.

As the day was beginning to wane, I pedaled on back out to US 70 toward my destination for the night. I would put in over fifty miles this day, a new record for me. I hardly noticed the forty-ish temperatures and my tired muscles.

**Even the pigs have character in Lebanon**

## A Slice of Tennessee

This bustling town of 20,235 exuded character. Even its name was distinctive—the pronunciation of the Middle Eastern country is LEB-uh-non; the locals here pronounced it LEB-uh-nun, or simply LEB-nun. Before this part of my ride ended, I would see mailboxes that looked like a motorcycle, a dog, and a hair dryer. I would see—honest-to-goodness—a large authentic-looking Statue of Liberty complete with an electric torch on its own island in somebody's large front yard pond. I would pass Snow White Barbecue and Pinky Pigglesworth plant nursery (with a huge pig statue welcoming the customers). And then there was the used car dealership with a 1940 Plymouth for sale for $5999, right alongside its later model vehicles (my Dad says such a car originally sold for $700).

Interesting. Distinctive. Did I say earlier that I thought the southern US 70 route from Crossville to Lebanon might prove boring? What was I thinking? This is Tennessee! The state has character!

**Character on display all around!**

*Chapter 7   Smithville to Lebanon*

***57.37 miles for the day***

***257.72 miles total***

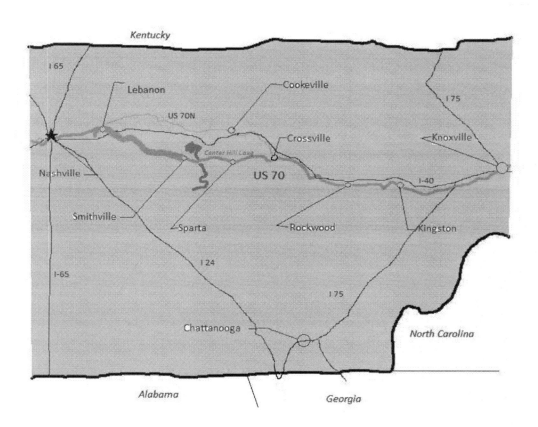

*A Slice of Tennessee*

# Chapter 8  Lebanon to Nashville
## New and Old

Good food and good company—nothing like it after pedaling fifty-seven miles.  The last twelve miles had depleted my last reserves of energy.  The clerk at Sleep Inn on State Highway 109 (four miles off of US 70) saw my bicycle and asked, "How far did you ride from?"  It felt so good to impress her with, "Smithville this morning, Crossville yesterday morning,"—all of it in weather quite chilly.  Yet it was bittersweet to see two other clerks hanging up Christmas garland in the lobby, a reminder of the rapidly approaching holiday (which I loved) and the interruption of my bike ride (which I hated).

A hot shower sure felt good and perked me up somewhat.  Not long after, I found myself seated in O'Charley's Restaurant, across from new friends, Jonas and Colleen Taylor.  Jonas pastored West Hills Baptist Church in Lebanon.  Ironically, what I discussed with my new friends was: old times.  Colleen and I had both attended Donelson High School in Nashville, one year apart.  She was

*A Slice of Tennessee*

in the same graduating class as my close friend Barry Chamberlain. He had put me into e-mail contact with her, said she had news media connections. Jonas had attended rival Two Rivers High School. We had several mutual friends from those days. But the small world gets smaller: years later, at different times, Jonas and I had each pastored on the Eastern Shore of Maryland at churches not half an hour apart. Colleen had edited a local newspaper there. New friends, old times—such a blend of new and old would characterize my ride the next day into Nashville.

Jonas and Colleen's son Peter joined us later at the restaurant. A student and football player at Tennessee Technological University, Peter had been plagued with injuries. Such misfortunes did not seem to dampen the spirits of this big young man in the least. Our fellowship across the meal was delightful. Afterward Jonas drove me back to my room. But first he took me by West Hills Church. His eyes seemed to burn in the darkness with his vision and passion for his people and the future of God's church in Lebanon. Who would have thought that Two Rivers High could produce such a godly church leader. (We always thought the worst of our rival.) All in all it was a blessed evening (Jonas even picked up the tab).

And to think—I would likely not have met such new/old friends if I had declined to mount my bicycle that misty rainy day outside of Newport two months earlier. Did I say I was the luckiest man in Tennessee? This evening only confirmed it.

It was a bone-chilling thirty degrees with light snow falling as I started out for Nashville the next morning. I was on the last leg of this three-day trip. And it would have to be my last trip until next spring and warmer weather. But what a ride it had been! I was on my Diamondback Crestview and I was going places! The thrill is in getting from *here* to *somewhere*, untethered, at bicycle speed. Arriving at a town, a historic sight, a memory, or a spectacular overlook

*Chapter 8   Lebanon to Nashville*

makes each day's ride a fresh experience.  I had a special sense of anticipation this day, for I was once again coming into familiar territory.

In 1968 Nashville became my home.  For six years we had lived in Knoxville and loved the area.  Dad looked forward to retiring there one day.  But while on vacation in Arizona during July of that year, we received the news from back home:  Dad had been offered an unexpected promotion, which would require relocation to Nashville.  Within a few weeks we were packed and moved to the city where I would graduate high school, meet my wife, and eventually be ordained as a minister.  In fact, I would soon ride past the house that knew me as a teenager, two buildings in downtown Nashville that knew me as a young engineer, and many other familiar sights from days gone by, *if* the city had not changed too much.

As I started up Hwy 109 back toward my old friend US 70, I caught a visual omen that somehow the old Nashville I knew and loved would still be present amidst the new and modern city streets and structures.  Across the highway was a Citgo gas station with a vaguely familiar design:  frame building with large picture windows and a long front porch.  Suddenly it hit me—I was looking at the original Cracker Barrel Restaurant!  In the early 1970's this business establishment was a novel idea, a restaurant coupled with an old country store.  Many a Sunday, Dad and Mom had taken us there after church for dinner.  I remembered now, they even sold gas back then.  The concept caught on rapidly, and as the chain grew and expanded, they dropped the gas market and gussied up their distinctive look.  Eventually they sold off this original store.  But it was still standing and triggered warm memories just the same.

*A Slice of Tennessee*

**The original Cracker Barrel Restaurant and Country Store**

Swinging back onto US 70, I kept my eyes peeled for the interesting, the unusual, the memorable. I wasn't disappointed. In fact, it's amazing how many unusual sights pass our eyes at motor vehicle speed that escape our notice. For instance, in a rural stretch between Lebanon and Mt. Juliet, there was a vacuum cleaner store located in a small, old remodeled house. But on the front porch, standing in a line as if at attention, was an array of colorful upright vacuum cleaners, some brand-spanking new and some old but refurbished. Another omen?

There was no "welcome to" sign for Mt. Juliet, but I knew I was there. It is built up, a growing, thriving area. I encountered the first bike traffic of my trans-state ride in this charming suburb of Nashville—a rider (complete with backpack, like me) just ahead of me, pedaling slower than I was. Should I be polite, I wondered, and slow down my already leisurely pace? Or should I give him a subtle hint by blasting my old-fashioned bulb bike horn? Neither. During a break in the increasing rush hour traffic, I pulled into the travel lane and passed around him. He wished me a good day. He looked as cold as I felt. In

*Chapter 8   Lebanon to Nashville*

my high school days there wasn't much rush hour traffic in Mt. Juliet. But within the next few years the creeping development from Nashville began to envelop this quiet town. It quickly became a bedroom community to the big city. At some point it took on a life of its own. I would be pedaling through built-up area all the way into downtown Nashville now.

Many new businesses lined the highway. Now and then I saw a store or shopping center I thought I recognized from days gone by. Some of them had morphed into new ones. Bill Crook's FoodTown was now Sav-A-Lot. The large red brick H. G. Hill's Food Store at the corner of Andrew Jackson Parkway is now a Dollar General Market. And Andrew Jackson Parkway itself was almost unrecognizable. Developers cut this road in 1969. The school bus I rode to DuPont High traveled over it to pick up a young girl way out in the sticks. Now, lined both sides with houses and commercial establishments its entire length, this median-divided short cut to Saundersville Road had likely not seen any sticks in many years. What about my old neighborhood in the suburb of Hermitage? What about Donelson and downtown Nashville itself? Would they too be so changed as to rob me of the pleasure of reminiscence as I pedaled through them?

My fears were alleviated on that score, for it seems that the more Nashville changes the more it stays the same. It is a unique blend of old and new, ancient and modern. Pedaling that morning into the community of Hermitage confirmed that delightful mix. The rural two-lane highway I remembered from my high school days is now multi-lane and developed all the way out to Mt. Juliet. Passing Shute Lane, however, I had the unsettling feeling that something was missing. Where was Rachel's Lane? Named for President Andrew Jackson's wife, this shady tree-lined country lane leads to the Hermitage, where Jackson and his wife made their home. Built in the early 1800's, this splendid mansion with the large white columns immediately transports the visitor back to horse and buggy days, even in the midst of the bustling metropolitan city.

I couldn't travel through here without giving this landmark a passing nod. But how was I to get there? The intersection with Rachel's Lane does not even exist anymore. The road runs under US 70 with a rustic split rail fence preventing vehicles and pedestrians (and bicycles?) from gaining access to it. Then I remembered: some years ago for reasons I still haven't figured out, the state eliminated this intersection and directed traffic to the Hermitage around Old Hickory Boulevard to the other end of Rachel's Lane. That route would take me a couple of miles out of my way. Surely there was an easier way to access this road. Then I saw it. On the opposite side of the highway a few of the rails had been knocked down at the far end of the bridge over Rachel's Lane. (Honest to goodness—I didn't do it!) I crossed the highway, lifted my Crestview over the downed rails, and eased it down the steep embankment. Voila! I was now on Rachel's Lane.

**Those rails were like that already!**

*Chapter 8    Lebanon to Nashville*

Pedaling down the road, large cow pastures on either side, I caught a glimpse of the mansion through the trees. It was about all the Hermitage I would be able to see that day. The huge cedar trees lining the graveled drive to the front of this elegant residence afforded only a limited view of the house itself. Nevertheless, it was exhilarating just to be in proximity to the place again. Many times I have toured the mansion and grounds, on occasion with visitors to our home. For the house we lived in after Dad was transferred to Nashville was just on the other side of the large pasture opposite the Hermitage driveway. Frequently my brother Johnny and I would hop the fence in our back yard, cross the pasture, and view what Hermitage we could for free from Rachel's Lane.

Andrew Jackson was one of three United States presidents from Tennessee, the other two being James Knox Polk and Andrew Johnson. A tough soldier and hero of the Battle of New Orleans, Jackson was one of our more colorful presidents. He had a hot temper and fought more than one duel, usually occasioned over his wife's honor. It seems that Rachel Donelson was not divorced from her estranged husband when she married Jackson (although she had received word that her divorce was indeed final). He built this mansion for Rachel, but was never able to spend much time there with her due to his political duties. Between his election to the White House and his inauguration, Rachel died of a heart attack. She was buried on Christmas Eve 1828 in her white inaugural gown. As I stood at the front gate, gazing down the driveway that had seen many a carriage, I tried to imagine away—just for a few moments—the bustling city of Nashville all around me and envision the world that ole Andrew knew in his day.

But again, Nashville is such a blend of the old and new that I could not remain in the distant past for long. The home that knew me as a high schooler was just down the road. I was eager to see if it had changed over the years. Despite the presence of new businesses on US 70—everything from car washes to chiropractic offices, fast food to pharmacies—the old neighborhood had

*A Slice of Tennessee*

changed surprisingly little. And the house at 355 Monaco Drive looked as if maybe four years had passed, not four decades. Only the presence of a small satellite dish bore witness to more recent times. (In 1968 the television choices were NBC, CBS, ABC, NPT, and one independent local station, Channel 17.)

The rest of the town of Hermitage, though, was almost unrecognizable from those old days. The once-two-lane highway sported only one fast food eatery back then, the Red Barn. The small FoodTown grocery store and Maxwell Drug Store anchored both ends of a small shopping center. What a buzz it caused in the community when a large Kroger food store opened at the corner of Jacksonian Drive. Now traffic and commerce thrived even on side roads.

All of which was why I so looked forward to crossing the old steel truss Elmer Disspayne Bridge over Stones River. A long-time local landmark, the bridge seemed to take upon itself the task of officially separating Donelson from Hermitage. Stones River is a small body of water that flows into the Cumberland River not far downstream from that bridge. Not far upstream is an Army Corps of Engineers dam that forms Priest Lake. My pal from high school, Barry Chamberlain, and I often swam and camped out along the edge of Priest Lake. Barry grew up about a quarter mile away from the river. He says that during the summer the water level was so low that it was possible to walk across it and keep your head dry. (I shivered at the thought of wading that river on this cold day.) My Dad says his father would occasionally bring him and his brother to a spot near here to swim when they were boys. They would cross a bridge that no longer exists; only a huge concrete abutment remains. Apparently the old structure met its demise when the state built the Disspayne bridge. One New Year's Eve Barry and I found ourselves down by the water's edge at midnight shooting off fireworks near the base of the old abutment. So even rivers and old bridges can hold fond memories for old sentimentalists.

Therefore you can understand my consternation at finding that the Disspayne Bridge had now been closed forever and all traffic diverted to the

*Chapter 8   Lebanon to Nashville*

newer but far less imaginative steel-reinforced concrete structure. State workers had already laid sod down in front of the old crossing in preparation for its demise. And to add insult to injury, they had even given the new bridge a new name—the Richard Harrington Bridge. How dare they! Why was I so angry at the prospect of the Disspayne Bridge's demolition? After all, didn't *it* replace the original bridge? But I didn't know the original bridge very well. I *knew* the Disspayne Bridge. The Disspayne Bridge was a good friend of mine. And you, sir, are no Disspayne Bridge! In a fit of pique, I refused to pedal across the new structure. Pushing my bike through the freshly laid sod, I proceeded over my old friend, past puzzled-looking laborers, and then back onto the highway.

**For decades it separated Donelson from Hermitage**

I was cold. I needed to rest a few minutes. I was still stewing over the calloused attitude of my state toward an old memory. Barry's folks still lived in the same house near the river. Perhaps I could get some physical and emotional warmth there. The Chamberlains were home and indeed provided plenty of both. Senior citizens tend to keep their houses quite warm, and on a thirty-degree morning, their house felt toasty. After the obligatory small talk, I lamented the demise of the Disspayne Bridge. "Why they're not tearing that bridge down," Mrs. Chamberlain explained, "they're going to leave it up for pedestrians." Wonderful! My spirits soared! Common sense had indeed prevailed! And it would be so typically Nashville—the combination of old and new. Remnants of the oldest bridge still standing; the second bridge left intact for pedestrians (and bicyclists?), and the newest bridge bearing the load of vehicular traffic. Alright, the state has a little more sense than I'd given them credit for.

**The Chamberlain's son Barry would finish the ride with me.**

*Chapter 8    Lebanon to Nashville*

It was always good to see the Chamberlains. They were laid back and gracious. After catching up on family and friends, I mentioned that my ride would take me past St. Thomas Hospital in the spring, on the other side of Nashville. We recalled the dark days I spent there wasting away from inflammatory bowel disease. Mr. Chamberlain had spent one whole afternoon there with me to keep me company. He even brought some papers from his office to work on while there; but we watched an episode of *The Big Valley*, and he didn't get much work done. Mr. and Mrs. Chamberlain were surprised to hear that it was Barry who had driven me to the hospital the night I was admitted.

Pedaling on into Donelson, my high school days began to flash before me. But unfortunately my old alma mater was hardly recognizable. I was privileged to be a member of the last graduating class at Donelson High School in 1971. The following year our school combined with our biggest rival Two Rivers High to form McGavock Comprehensive High. Good old DHS morphed into a junior high school. Later massive renovations took out the old gymnasium and many of the old familiar classrooms. Thankfully, memories remain even after edifices pass away.

Soon I passed by a discount grocery, formerly the H. G. Hills store I worked in as a teenager. In those days we routinely carried out a customer's groceries and even placed them into their vehicle. Sometimes they tipped us for the service. My favorite tip was the four silver dimes a man gave me one evening. Usually I'd make enough in tips on Saturday to pay for my lunch at nearby Shoneys. A café now, this Shoneys was a thriving business at that time. It even had curb service, where every Friday and Saturday night teens would cruise around looking for something to happen (nothing ever did).

The ride on toward town revealed Dick's Flowers, still in business almost forty years after I bought Marcia her first roses for Valentine's Day—seven, one for each month we'd been dating. Dick's people even delivered them. A little further I encountered remnants of the "S" curves of Lebanon Road, long since

*A Slice of Tennessee*

straightened out. A set of concrete steps leading from the shoulder up to a long vacant lot suggested a residential area predating the current commercial build-up.

I was jarred back to reality as I glanced up at a billboard advertising "the first touch-screen Blackberry." High technology during my days at the Hills store consisted of black land line telephones and the latest modern marvel: eight track tape players.

Entering the downtown area, I rode past a modern bridge over the Cumberland River which replaced the old Shelby Street Bridge near the Tennessee Titan's football stadium. Here again common sense prevailed: the old bridge had been preserved for pedestrians. Remnants of the old amidst the new. Next I arrived at Broadway, Nashville's long-time main street. In 1779 James Robertson brought a party of settlers down the Cumberland River. Legend has it that they arrived on Christmas Day and crossed the frozen-solid river right here. Perhaps they saw the Purina feed and fertilizer store on the corner. Or maybe Tootsie's Orchid Lounge a few blocks up looked inviting. Could it have been the strains of country music they heard from the Ryman Auditorium? Alright, those establishments would arrive much later, but for whatever reason, these pioneers chose this spot for their new settlement.

Standing near the river bank and looking up Broadway, I marveled at the modern skyscrapers, the sports arena, the convention center—intermingling with vintage Nashville landmarks. Again, old amidst the new. Locals even frequently refer to this street by its original name, Broad Street.

I would finish this leg of my ride at Eighth and Broad. It had been a cold day with the promise of many more ahead. I would have to wait for the first warm weather of spring to continue from downtown Nashville and beyond. But first I had to check out two local downtown landmarks.

*Chapter 8   Lebanon to Nashville*

**Old or new, they are engineering marvels.**


The State Capitol Building reminds visitors and locals that Nashville is the Athens of the South.  Designed ca. 1845 by prominent nineteenth century architect William Strickland (who is interred within its walls), this unique Greek revival edifice has four Ionic porticoes and a Doric basement.  Rumor has it that Tennessee residents insisted that, Greek design or no, their Capitol must have a dome or tower like other state capitol buildings; hence, the square tower with the round cupola on top.  Ancient Greek culture combined with modern southern culture in one building—again, a symbol of the old and new in Nashville.

A grand marble stairway graces the inside of the Capitol.  These steps have conveyed many a legislator and spectator from the main floor to the legislative chambers, not only providing elevation but also bearing witness to colorful history.  In 1866 Tennessee lawmakers sat poised to vote on readmission to the Union, the first state to do so.  Two representatives, however, were not thrilled with that prospect and exited the chambers before the vote. Their presence was necessary for a quorum.  Therefore, the Sergeant-at-Arms ordered them back into the room.  When they failed to heed his command and started down the marble steps, this officer promptly took aim and fired his weapon in their direction, halting their retreat. They grudgingly returned to the chambers, and Tennessee was readmitted to the Union. Several years ago I was showing a friend the chipped marble banister, a permanent souvenir of the incident. Following the trajectory to a nearby marble column, we were excited to discover the bullet still lodged there, a mute witness to wilder days, more desperate times.

**Nashvillians *had* to have that cupola on top!**

The other landmark I sought out was a more personal one: First Baptist Church. Founded in 1820 the church has had a long and fascinating history. At one point during the mid-1800's, a persuasive pastor coaxed and cajoled the

*Chapter 8    Lebanon to Nashville*

entire congregation into leaving the Baptist denomination and becoming Church of Christ.  Five members met on the courthouse steps shortly afterward to reconstitute First Baptist Church and keep it going.  Such strong pulpiteers as J. R. Graves, W. H. Powell, and H. Franklin Paschall have graced this church's sanctuary.

Staff member and long-time friend Sandra Gentry arranged to let me into the building to take some pictures for auld lang syne.  Parts of the structure had been renovated to the point that I barely knew where I was.  The entire back entrance had been remodeled.  Was this the stairwell I ascended every Sunday morning to the Senior High Sunday School Department?  One rainy Sunday morning, before our teacher arrived, Dorris Charlton, Ken Kautzman, and I took turns dropping little paper cups of punch out the window of our classroom three stories to the parking lot below.  Dorris succeeded in hitting a car parked next to Dr. Paschall's.  The rain quickly washed away the evidence.

The sanctuary looked the same as it did when completed in 1970.  Almost forty years old, this auditorium nevertheless still looked quite modern.  Dr. Paschall married Marcia and me in that cavernous room in 1975.  (Resplendent in my white tuxedo, I looked—according to my brother-in-law— like a nervous Rhett Butler on that occasion.)  The earlier 1886 building was literally falling apart when the church voted to build a new sanctuary, much to the dismay of some of the old guard members.  But in a spirit of unity, the spire from the original building remained and was incorporated into the design of the new building.  What a fitting addition to the skyline of Nashville, a city that so blends the old with the new.

**1886 and 1970 brought together in one building**

On a lark I circled the downtown before heading south off my appointed US 70 route to my lodging for the evening. Stopping in at a trendy coffee shop in the old Doctor's Building, I savored a delightful hot chocolate and roast beef sandwich. A smartly dressed man of about twenty-five years sat near me, and we engaged in some pleasant conversation. Ashford grew up in Knoxville (as did I) but now worked in the state's capital for the Democratic Party. He was bright, articulate, had a promising future, I thought. Years earlier I myself had been a young engineer, working for the Tennessee Department of Transportation in this very building. Many years prior to that, my Dad had come to the building as a lad to have his tonsils removed. My how times change! In

*Chapter 8    Lebanon to Nashville*

Dad's day African-Americans could not even eat at the white lunch counter on this very street.  In the 1960's a sit-in had changed that policy.  And now this upwardly-mobile African-American party worker was sharing conversation with me in an old building full of memories.  Old amidst the new.

I pedaled south several miles to stay at my mother-in-law's house for the night and to await Marcia's arrival.  I passed more history en route:  the huge reservoir built about the time of Noah's flood (actually 1889) and still serving the city today.  It holds 51,000,000 gallons of water in two basins.  In 1912 the reservoir sponsored its own flood:  a wall gave way, spilling the 26,000,000 gallons out of one basin, washing away houses and trees for several city blocks.  Miraculously, no one was killed.  I pedaled by this Nashville landmark quickly, looking up as I passed.

A short detour took me to Honeycutt Engineering, my brother-in-law's consulting engineering firm .  In the 1980's Wilburn came to work in the company, which his father Sam had started decades earlier.  Never wanting to retire, Sam had worked in that office as long as he was physically able.  But by the time of my ride, he was living out his final days at a Nashville hospital.  Wilburn kept a bookshelf in his outer office where he proudly displayed tools of his father's trade which have now been replaced by computerized instruments.  Again, old amid the new.

A few minutes later, another short detour took me by the Governor's mansion on South Curtiswood Lane, just off the main highway.  The late Minnie Pearl (Mrs. Henry Cannon) had lived next door and was a good friend and neighbor to every new occupant of the mansion.  My wife had had a brief encounter once as a teenager with the delightful Minnie.  She, her mother, and her sister Nancy were exiting a grocery store parking lot on Franklin Road when they spied Minnie herself (disguised as a sensible and proper Mrs. Cannon) entering the store.  They rolled down the car windows and shouted, "Hello, Minnie Pearl!"  Whereupon, the sedate Mrs. Cannon turned on her heel, waved at them, and shouted back her trademark "Howdee!"

*A Slice of Tennessee*

**An old stone wall, probably built with slave labor, along busy Franklin Road**

    This ride was over all too soon as I neared my mother-in-law's house in Brentwood. To savor it just a little longer, I stopped at a nearby Starbucks for another hot chocolate (so good on a cold afternoon!). But then I had to face facts: winter had now arrived. I would be stuck for awhile at Eighth and Broad in Nashville. But just wait till spring! I would be back on my Diamondback Crestview (or so I thought) and riding (and writing) again. I had had only enough of my slice of Tennessee to whet my appetite for more!

*Chapter 8   Lebanon to Nashville*

**46.37 miles for the day**

**304.09 miles total**

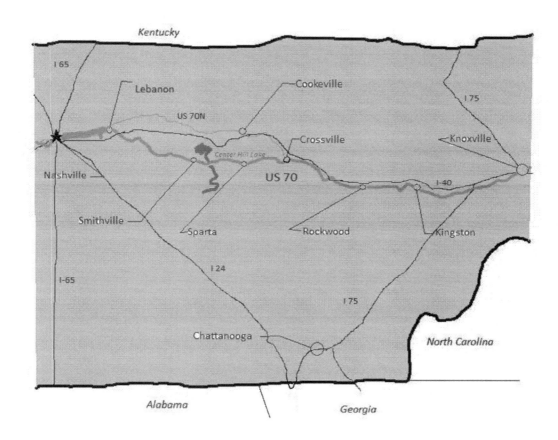

*A Slice of Tennessee*

## Chapter 9  Goodbye to an Old Friend

Alright.  I know it was just an inanimate object.  I admit it.  But it felt like an old and reliable friend.  And I still miss it.

*It* is my Diamondback Crestview hybrid bicycle.  Affectionately referred to here as *The Bike*, this vehicle was a near constant companion for almost seven years.  We had some marvelous adventures together.  Like Johnny Cash, "We've been everywhere, man" (well, almost).

*A Slice of Tennessee*

The Bike and I saw Cape Hatteras and Okracoke Island together. We actually arrived there in a little Cessna, piloted by my good deacon friend Jim Thompson. We wound our way around the nation's capital on at least three occasions, looking at the cherry blossoms or going to the Library of Congress to do research. We went camping together in Tennessee and enjoyed long rides around Topsail Island, North Carolina, during a family reunion trip. One Memorial Day holiday my good preacher friend Lon Chenowith and I pedaled from my house in Caryville, Tennessee, to Cumberland Gap on the Tennessee/Kentucky/Virginia line (about forty-three miles away).

My Diamondback even navigated Bike New York like a pro. Jim Thompson and another deacon friend, Matt Wallace, rode with us on that one—forty-five miles with 30,000 other bikers through all five boroughs of New York City. That was the one time the old girl let me down. In the middle of Central Park, suddenly and inexplicably the rear derailleur disintegrated, damaging the rear wheel and bending the frame. By the grace of God, we found an open bicycle repair shop some blocks away from the bike route. They fixed the damage quickly, and we rejoined the pack of bikers and finished the tour.

Originally, I rode a one speed cruiser bike with coaster brakes. I bought it used from a bike rental dealer near where I pastored in Maryland. I would ride several miles a day out Deal Island Road or Mount Vernon Road for regular exercise and stress relief and to keep from becoming a fat preacher. The cruiser bike worked well in the flat terrain of the Eastern Shore. But one Sunday afternoon, I ran into Matt Wallace and his wife Gretchen out riding their new hybrid bicycles. I stopped to admire their recent acquisitions, then continued down the road on my one speed cruiser. A couple of months later, upon returning from a mission trip to Sandy Valley, Nevada, I discovered The Bike sitting in my living room, a gift from Matt. I gave away the cruiser, and The Bike and I became fast friends. Matt probably does not realize even now what a blessing The Bike has been to me.

*Chapter 9   Goodbye to an Old Friend*

But by the time I arrived in Nashville on my trans-state ride, the old Diamondback was complaining more and more frequently—slipping gears, worn brakes, broken spokes, sluggish shifting—not at all like the early days of effortless, quiet shifting and smooth riding. Well, 9000-10,000 miles (my best estimate) is a lot to put on any bike. Even the dealer-repairman in Knoxville was impressed. However, to repair, adjust, and outfit the old girl for more years of service put me in the price range of a new bike with the benefit of more recent design changes. So I acquired a Specialized Globe to take up where the Diamondback Crestview left off. It would prove the beginning of many new adventures. But I still felt a twinge of sadness putting the old girl out to pasture. After all, she got me half way across the state on my "Slice of Tennessee" ride!

*A Slice of Tennessee*

# Chapter 10 Nashville to Dickson
# A Ninety-Degree Bend in the Road

*" For lo, the winter is past, the rain is over and gone. The flowers appear on the earth; the time of singing has come, and the voice of the turtledove is heard in our land"* (Song of Solomon 2:11-12) [NKJV].

It was finally spring! I could ride again! I had a partner this time! We would leave out of downtown Nashville, right where I had left off at Eighth and Broad.

It was not a bright, sunny day. In fact, there were a few clouds on the horizon, literally and figuratively. Already I was pondering our first stop that day—St. Thomas Hospital. My mind began to drift back to the fall of 1975.

"You're doing great, Bill!" said Dr. Smith. I didn't feel great. In fact, I felt like a wrecked car on its terminal trip to the salvage yard. The future looked bleak, uncertain. As I strained to see ahead, life looked like a dead end street.

*A Slice of Tennessee*

Barely two months into my new married life with Marcia, a long-smoldering inflammatory bowel disease had suddenly burst into flame, putting me into St. Thomas Hospital for a ten week tenure of more pain and sickness than I had ever experienced. Drs. Richard Schneider and Roy Elam, excellent physicians both, had struggled to no avail to bring me into remission as I wasted away to a skeletal wraith of my former self. Finally, they had called in Dr. Daugh Smith to perform life-saving surgery. It would be a long recovery.

Dr. Smith was an experienced surgeon. He was also brutally honest, no-nonsense, even gruff. At the time he performed the operation on my sickly 107-pound body, he himself—at age seventy—was recuperating from an auto accident. He still wore a large metal brace about his chest. He was a heavy smoker. Nothing seemed to stop him. And just three weeks after the surgery, he was adamant that I was doing well. "Bill, the day I operated on you, you had one foot in the grave! You wouldn't be alive now if we hadn't operated when we did! You just need time to heal," he insisted, almost angrily.

Maybe he was right. Maybe the *end* of the road up ahead was really just a ninety degree *bend* in the road.

Those dark, uncertain days were now but a distant memory. How ironic that at age fifty-five I would find myself not only riding my bicycle the length of Tennessee but also riding right past the very hospital where I lay languishing so many years ago. Preparing for this segment of the ride, a plan had suddenly come into focus: why not have a brief celebration on the front lawn of the hospital as I rode past it? Family and friends could be present, and if I could interest the local media, it could turn into a real event.

But this opportunity seemed determined to be wasted. I had contacted some local news outlets and a lot of friends with possible ties to the media, but no one seemed interested. Was this ride really about media attention, though? Wasn't it for the thrill of the ride? Wasn't it enough that I could ride by that

*Chapter 10   Nashville to  Dickson*

hospital in triumph?  We invited a few family members to be present on the lawn of the hospital.  That would be satisfaction enough.  Unknown to me, however, Marcia had been working on my behalf.  She had contacted hospital personnel and explained to them the celebration I had planned, asking if some representative of the hospital could be present when I arrived.  They were indeed interested; the facility had its own quarterly publication for its 1800 employees, and the administration believed it was good for morale periodically to publish St. Thomas "success" stories.  That was the kind of publicity I really wanted anyway.  Two officials would meet us out front.

A week prior to setting out, I had found phone numbers for Drs. Schneider and Elam (both serving at Vanderbilt Medical Center).  These two gracious and competent physicians, along with the late Dr. Smith, attended my case and helped save my life in 1975.  I had not talked with either one in many years.  Yet each seemed eager to speak with me as I called.  How good it felt to tell these men about my bike-riding project and the health I now enjoyed.  They both had conflicts and could not attend the hospital-front-lawn celebration; however, they were delighted with my project and wished me well.

My bike ride across the state of Tennessee had ended for the winter in November at the intersection of Eighth Avenue and Broadway in downtown Nashville.  Now on this cloudy March Monday morning, I was beginning again. While I was eager to get started, the day ahead was fraught with uncertainties. Would the rain hold off?  Could we make it the five miles to the hospital for our 8:45 am celebration without being stopped by a flat tire (a common problem on major city streets)?  The hospital officials had a narrow window of time before another important meeting.  Would anyone even be present besides Marcia?  A new aspect of this ride was my partner Josh.  Living in Ohio, he was not used to pedaling the rolling hills of Middle Tennessee.  Could we make our ultimate destinations of Montgomery Bell State Park that afternoon and Waverly the next day?

**It was good to have a riding partner at last**

Marcia and her mother dropped off Josh and me and our bicycles in a parking lot near Eighth and Broad. The sky was cloudy but not dark. The temperature was in the mid-fifties. My orange and white University of Tennessee sweatshirt would keep me plenty warm in the cool morning air. As we reinstalled our quick-release front wheels, I was bubbling over with excitement. But I had an eye on the time. We had less than twenty minutes to make our rendezvous with the gentlemen from St. Thomas Hospital. We started out in moderately heavy traffic, weaving our way past Vanderbilt University's campus and the modern hotels and restaurants as well as the few remaining stately old mansions on West End Avenue. The tires were holding up alright despite the debris littering the parking lane we were riding in. I pedaled fast, Josh staying close behind me. In no time we were crossing over I-440 Parkway, and then there it was—St. Thomas. A long established landmark now, it was brand new in 1975 when I entered as a patient.

We pedaled up to the front emergency room entrance. My lands! Was it thirty-three years earlier that Barry Chamberlain had driven me up to this very spot, so sick that I could hardly stand? That night Marcia's cousin Dr. Will Ralph, a prominent Nashville allergist, met us at the hospital and admitted me. My family physician had been reluctant to do so for reasons unknown to me to this day. But Will knew how sick I was and told Marcia, "Get Bill down to St. Thomas *tonight*, and I'll admit him." A day or two earlier I had been afraid that Will was miffed at me—he had planned an elaborate backyard barbecue bash at his house in honor of my recent marriage to Marcia. But we had cancelled out just two days prior to the event because I was just that sick. Then here he was, the very night he had planned on hosting this party in our honor, admitting me to St. Thomas. At least he could see my illness firsthand. (He's another one I probably ought to credit with saving my life.)

**Skinny and frail after my 1975 surgery**

What a thrill it was to pedal my bicycle up that hospital driveway! Paul Lindsley (Director of Communications) and Jerome R. (Jerry) Kearney (Vice President of Mission), true to their word, were waiting for us, smiling. Marcia and her mother were already there, waving, pointing, and shouting, "Here they come." And to my surprise and delight, my son-in-law Matt was standing with them, as well as my sister-in-law Susan Honeycutt. Marcia was carrying the enormous scrapbook filled with dozens of cards and letters from family and friends from 1975. During my ten-week tenure at St. Thomas, pasting those cards in that book had helped me maintain my sanity. Now they are precious to go back and pore over. I pointed out one of Susan's cards that she had sent me thirty-three years earlier in which she was updating me on the progress of Tennessee Vols football. (Football loyalties never change.) The moment was special, as Paul interviewed me for the hospital publication and everyone was snapping pictures. I passed around an old photograph of my own, the only one I could find from my era of sickness. Taken approximately three months after the surgery, the picture revealed a ghostly but smiling character with long thinning hair (from the powerful medications I was taking), clad in overalls (the only comfortable clothing I could find to hang on my bony frame). My lands, again! Was I ever that skinny and sickly? I was suddenly appreciative of my fifty-five-year old health and vigor.

**A true St. Thomas success story**

*Chapter 10   Nashville to Dickson*

We said our thanks (especially to the Lord) and our goodbyes and pushed on. My fears for the day were rapidly flying the coop. The celebration had certainly elevated my spirits. I told Josh we could now ride at a more leisurely pace. We had all day to reach the state park. As we continued out Harding Road (US 70S), I pointed out an apartment complex that Barry had helped to build one summer during our college days. It was during that time that he bought his first car, a small brown Dodge Dart. That lasted him a year or so till he could get a more manly blue Ford F-100 pickup.

A little further out we passed Belle Meade Plantations. John Harding of Virginia bought this 250-acre tract of land along the Natchez Trace in 1807 and used it to board horses, raise thoroughbreds, and grow and ship grain to ports as far away as Charleston and New Orleans. His son William built the mansion in 1853 that still stands today. That structure suffered through the Battle of Nashville, with Union and Confederate forces skirmishing on the front lawn.

**Forerunner to Belle Meade Mansion?**

*A Slice of Tennessee*

The stately columns are riddled with bullets to this day. The mansion also survived a severe financial downturn at the beginning of the twentieth century, in which the fourth generation of Hardings sold the property. In 1953 a historical society acquired the plantation and turned it into a museum.

I noticed that there were still clouds on the horizon and the distinct possibility of rain. Riding in the rain is no fun (well, riding across Tennessee in *any* kind of weather was a blast, but dry blasts are so much more pleasant than wet blasts). And a figurative cloud had appeared now, a problem I was becoming increasingly concerned about: Josh was slowing down. Especially on the steeper hills. I had forgotten about his knee injury from playing football a couple of years earlier. Tennessee grades were taking more of a toll on it than flat Ohio roads. And the dreaded "Nine Mile Hill" loomed a short distance ahead. The very name filled me with trepidation. Was it nine miles from the bottom to the top, steep upgrade all the way? Surely not, but maybe they named it that because it seemed nine miles long. I hoped I could pedal it, but I was used to Tennessee hills. Josh was younger and stronger than I but *not* used to steep grades. My Dad's words now came back to me: "It *ain't* all downhill to Memphis." My biggest fear was that Josh would get discouraged, call Marcia to pick him up, and I'd lose my pedaling partner. Just one more uncertainty for the day.

We pedaled up one not-so-steep hill after another; they were quite do-able. At the crest of one such upgrade, I happened to notice a green-and-white mile marker—it contained one digit: nine. It hit me like a jolt. *This* was Nine Mile Hill! It was not nine miles of upgrade. It was nine miles out from town. We had topped it and lived to tell about it!

With Nine Mile Hill conquered, the built-up area of Nashville's suburban district was finally beginning to thin out. The day, though still overcast, was turning out to be mild and dry. Check off one more uncertainty—rain. But others still loomed ahead.

*Chapter 10   Nashville to Dickson*

Soon the highway narrowed to two lanes and began a slow, curvy climb, hugging the muddy Harpeth River on our left as it went. Pretty scenary, but would the hills ever flatten out? Josh's bike didn't take the grades as readily as mine. He fell behind a little more with each hill. I was beginning to wonder how he would feel about another day of riding.

I pulled over to rest and let Josh catch up. Suddenly from behind us a long funeral procession approached. We stood on the shoulder till it passed. I didn't have to tell Josh to take off his helmet; he even held it over his heart. That's my son.

**Seems like it ought to have a bigger sign**

We wound our way through the community of Pegram and soon passed the turn-off to the Narrows of the Harpeth State Natural Area. Montgomery Bell, whose namesake park would host Josh and me that night, operated a forge

*A Slice of Tennessee*

in a horseshoe bend of the river as early as 1820. To harness water power for his ironworks, he had slave laborers blast out a tunnel one hundred yards long through the limestone bedrock of a ridge to allow water of the Harpeth to flow from one side of the seven-mile bend to the other. Bell was a manufacturer and entrepreneur, who contributed greatly to the economic development of Middle Tennessee. Originally from Chester County, Pennsylvania, Bell gravitated to Tennessee for its abundance of iron ores and streams conducive to milling operations. Upon his death he left $20,000 to establish a boys' school, which remains to this day: Montgomery Bell Academy. All that remains of his forge today is the tunnel and a slag pond.

Yet, the horseshoe bend, tunnel, pond and ridge are now preserved as a state natural area and well worth an afternoon's visit. Some years before the state acquired the site, my college buddy John Claxton and I camped out in a tent on top of that ridge. A certain spot beyond our camp afforded a breath-taking view of the Harpeth Valley below. It was mesmerizing to watch the setting suns last rays washing over the rich farmland below and hearing in the far distance a local farmer calling in his cows. One morning I crept out of the tent early to see the view at daylight. I could hear the farmer calling to his cows again. His work must have involved long days. Hearing the brush rustling to my right, I looked up and saw a red fox scampering away. I wondered if Montgomery Bell ever took the time to enjoy such scenes during his day.

Years later I would visit this same site with Marcia and the kids, including Josh. I showed them the spot where John and I had camped and the scenic overlook. I described the red fox, took them through the tunnel, and let them see the slag pond. Before we left we found a trilobite fossil on the ground. Now Josh and I were in the area again on an all-new adventure. The Narrows of the Harpeth now hold three separate sets of warm memories for me.

We pedaled on through lonely wooded countryside punctuated by yellow jonquils in full bloom, a sign of both the past and the future—the past, because they reminded the passersby of the long-gone homes they once decorated; the future, because they were a sure sign that spring was close at hand.

**Three sets of memories at the Narrows**

      Still about six miles shy of White Bluff, we stopped a few minutes, ostensibly to check our map. The day was warming up. Our pedaling was generating body heat. Lunch is always a highlight of a biking day. It not only provides a break from pedaling and needed nourishment and refreshment, but it also affords a close-up look at another town, its charm, its character. This day I was looking ahead to the town of White Bluff and an exciting lunch for an additional reason: I was becoming increasingly concerned that Josh was perhaps not enjoying this ride and would drop out that day. We both knew there were plenty more hills between Nashville and Waverly. And I so wanted

Josh to make it to Waverly with me the next day to meet the cousin we'd never known previously and see where our ancestor Dr. Horner had lived.

**The jonquil: a harbinger of spring in Tennessee**

A grizzled local man of about sixty approached us on the roadside. He saw us looking at a map (trying to find something on it that said White Bluff was closer than we thought). He graciously asked if we needed directions. His name was Johnny. I confessed to him that the primary purpose of our stop was rest. He seemed to like that. We did take the opportunity to ask him a question we would ask frequently after that: was the road ahead hilly or flat? He told us it was "uphill both ways" to White Bluff. I was almost afraid to ask about eateries there. White Bluff was not a big place—what if there was no place to eat? But he assured us that a good Mexican restaurant awaited us. I hoped so. My only previous recollection of the town was from my high school days when we passed through there on a long trip, pulling a pop-up camper behind our car. We had eaten lunch in a diner only to come out afterward and discover that someone had stolen the spare tire off the back of our camper.

*Chapter 10   Nashville to  Dickson*

Three of the six miles passed on by.  We were looking for White Bluff around each curve, at the top of each rise.  On our left we spotted a man waving at us from a pickup truck in a hardware store parking lot.  It was Johnny.  Funny how you can feel such a kinship with someone you met for just a brief few minutes.

Johnny was right.  White Bluff was uphill both ways, and it did indeed have a good Mexican restaurant.  El Monte Restaurante looked right promising: plain exterior, full parking lot, exotic aromas wafting through the front door.  And it certainly lived up to its recommendation.  After thirty miles of pedaling Josh and I were sitting at the table wolfing down sizzling fajitas and drinking cold tea.  It's funny how the body and spirit can rebound after just a brief few minutes at a good restaurant.  We were amused at some of the local good ole boys' attempts to communicate with the *meseros* waiting the tables.  "Fway-go! Mooey cally-entay!" they exclaimed in mock protest, pointing at their enchiladas.

Our delightful Latin dining experience was spoiled, however, as we mounted up and began to pedal off.  I had noticed earlier that workers were busy reconstructing a portion of the restaurant building, and I had tried to be extra careful not to pedal over loose nails, staples, or other debris.  But suddenly I heard and felt that sickening *bump, bump, bump*—a flat tire, my third since starting down the mountain that rainy morning outside of Newport six months earlier.  Normally a flat is just a minor annoyance, a fifteen-minute fix.  This one would prove to be a threat to this segment of my trans-state ride.

Initially I saw this flat as a learning experience for Josh.  He could see his dad swap out tubes to get the bike ride-able again, then find the leak and patch it, thus providing the spare for my next flat.  But it's axiomatic:  whenever you are trying to impress one of your grown children, you will invariably do something wrong.  I thought the tire was tubed, inflated, and raring to go.  But as we started out, I still felt that sickening *bump, bump, bump*.  Close examination revealed that the tire was badly out of round.  It seemed to be properly inflated.  It did not appear to be binding anywhere around the rim.  I was stumped. I'd changed dozens of flats but never seen anything like this—but of course my son was watching now. Montgomery Bell State Park was just a few miles away. We limped along. We'd make the park, but I had no idea how to fix the problem. And there was not an overabundance of bicycle repair shops in the area.

Meanwhile, we encountered another challenge at the entrance to Montgomery Bell. The park road forked just past the entrance—nice flat roads!—and the turnoff to the Inn was to our left. We had not advanced fifty yards after turning when the road suddenly turned into a long steep upgrade. And I mean *steep.* Up, up, and away! For a solid mile! Soon we were both walking our bikes. We were exhausted. Josh had tackled hills he could not have prepared for. My back tire was bumping on its flat spot. Talk about uncertainty. I knew we would reach the Inn, but I was also sure this upgrade would be the straw to break the camel's back for Josh. He had not complained all day, but I doubted he would relish another day straining against such hills. And I doubted seriously that my bike would even be ride-able.

**More surprises awaited us after we arrived at the Park**

*Chapter 10    Nashville to  Dickson*

The Inn at Montgomery Bell is truly a work of art.  Built into the side of a large hill, it's back side, complete with balconies on every room, looks out over the lake, trees, and wildlife.  It's not unusual to see a beaver slide on down the slope into the water.  Turtles, squirrels, and other fun creatures abound.  I was looking forward to relaxing in this haven.  Back home in Campbell County the head ranger at our local Cove Lake State Park, Ranger Kim Moore, had shown interest in my bike ride from the first.  He was raised on the grounds of Montgomery Bell Park, his mother having been a manager there.  Ranger had arranged reservations for Josh and me, as he was still well-acquainted with the current manager of the Inn.  (As it turns out, Ranger had even covered the price of the room for us.)  It's nice to walk in where the management expects you.

But unfortunately the desk clerk at the Inn could not find our reservation.  I asked to see the manager (as Ranger had instructed me to do if there were any problem).  But the clerk told me brusquely, "She's not here today."  As I was beginning to show my irritation with flat tires, unexpected hills, and lost reservations, the clerk told us there were plenty of rooms anyway, and she fixed us up with one.  I cooled down.  The room even had a nice view of the lake.  (The mix-up was on Montgomery Bell's end, and Ranger felt terrible about it when I told him later.  He made sure they did not charge me for the room.)

Josh and I enjoyed walking the grounds, tired though we were.  I recalled some of the numerous times I had camped or picnicked with family and friends here.  When Marcia and I had married thirty-four years earlier, my grandmother had given us a nice canvas tent for a wedding gift.  Our first camping trip with it (the first of many through the years) was just a few weeks later on the Fourth of July at this very park.

I soon discovered that Josh had some memories of his own.  On more than one occasion we had joined some homeschooling friends in camping at this park.  And Josh recollected one warm summer day in his teen years that our friends Georgia Reeves and Janet Herbert had brought him and friends Adam and John Paul up here to swim, ride the paddle boats, and hike.

We enjoyed a meal in the Inn's restaurant; I had forgotten what an elegant dining room it was. Then returning to our room, I took some pictures off our balcony while Josh settled in to watch his favorite show, *24.* Jack Bauer was in big trouble (as usual), but somehow at the end of the twenty-four hours, he would, we suspected, be alive to fight another day.

I couldn't enjoy the show much, though, for trying to fix my back tire. I deflated it, inflated it, worked with it, all to no avail. I even called The Bike Zoo in Knoxville. They had sold me the bike a few months earlier, and Jeff tried long distance to diagnose the problem and suggest a fix. I would need to get to a more powerful air pump somewhere and keep deflating and inflating—carefully—while massaging the tire. I would not know until the next day, then, if I could fix it. I didn't even know where the nearest gas station with a pump was—or how many quarters it would take.

**The view from our room was worth all the pedaling**

*Chapter 10    Nashville to  Dickson*

So the day that started with significant uncertainties ended with the same.

I suggested to Josh that Marcia could drive out and pick him up the next morning.  He shocked me by asserting resolutely, "I want to try to make it to Waverly."  He had trained for this ride.  He didn't want to let a few hills stop him.  I couldn't believe my ears!  Maybe Jack Bauer had inspired him.  Wonderful!

And if he was willing to ride one more day after all he'd been through, surely I could bump, bump, bump my way into another town and perhaps find a way to fix my tire.  Maybe that *end* of the road ahead really was just a *bend* in the road.  The next morning would tell.

**Ode to a Flat**
(With Apologies to Joyce Kilmer)

**I think that I shall never see**
**A bike tire entirely puncture free.**

**A tire whose shrader valve can rest**
**From inflating after each puncture-pest.**

**A tire that can look just fine all day**
**Without suddenly going flat all the way.**

**A tire that has a lot of wear,**
**Yet not a single patch doth bear.**

**Upon whose tread there is no rain**
**While changing the tube—such a pain!**

**I should leave verse to poets like Joyce K.,**
**But flat or no, a bike ride makes my day!**

*A Slice of Tennessee*

**36.63 miles for the day**

**340.72 miles total**

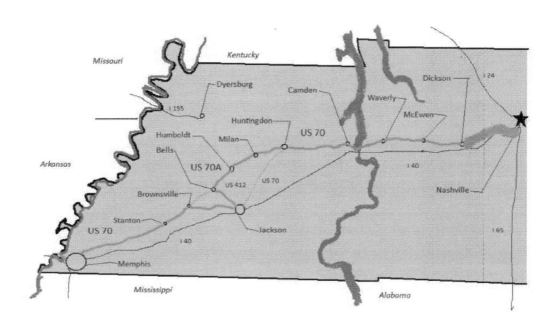

## Chapter 11  Dickson to Camden
## Roots and Wings

Roots and wings—those are two gifts all parents should bestow on their children.  And roots and wings were on my mind as Josh and I started out from Montgomery Bell State Park the next morning, a bright, sunshiny day with the temperature in the fifties.  It was a perfect spring morning for riding.  Despite the troubles of Monday, our spirits soared.  We were riding!  We were beginning here and going—somewhere.  If we hit more trouble, Marcia could come fetch us.  Besides, a bad day bike riding is better than a good day working.

Recently Marcia had dined with her brother Wilburn and his wife Susan at a restaurant in Nashville.  They were recalling family memories in the wake of their father's recent passing.  Wilburn observed the value of giving our children roots, i.e., a family heritage and values.  But it is equally important, he continued, that parents also give their children wings, i.e., permission and blessing to leave home, pursue their goals, and stand on their own two feet.

*A Slice of Tennessee*

Cutting the young ones loose involves risk; but if a foundation of family heritage and godly values is established early, the rewards far outweigh the risks. Josh and I would reconnect with some of our roots while enjoying the fruits of our wings on our second day of riding together.

Our soaring spirits notwithstanding, we still had a significant problem to overcome. Plan A was to look for a bicycle shop in Dickson. Perhaps they could fix my out-of-round back tire. Although Dickson is not a large town, we did not even know where to begin looking. So we swallowed our manly pride and asked directions. We began with our waitress at the High Point Diner.

Breakfast on the road is usually a treat, and this morning was no disappointment. The diner had the thickest, best tasting pancakes I'd had in quite awhile. The bacon also was nice and thick—I could sink my teeth into it. Our waitress, a number of years my senior, did not seem too friendly at first. Was she just busy, or was it that Josh and I were obviously not locals? She did warm up about halfway through our meal. (I have found that sprinkling a few sincere "thank yous" and "ma'ams" sometimes helps to break the ice.) I asked her if she knew of a bicycle shop in town. No, she told us wanting to help, but her brother Carl sitting at a nearby table might. Alas, even Carl did not know of one in the area. However, between bites of biscuits and gravy, this massive, white-haired man did encourage us with the news that the hills would flatten out within a few miles.

So it was that we were reduced to Plan B. Plan B was to find a gas station with an air hose—not one of those that you feed quarters while it dribbles out air, but one with some real power behind it—and keep deflating and inflating the tire, while massaging it, till the flat spot popped out. But on our route I spied no such station. So I bump, bump, bumped all the way to McEwen, about fifteen miles away. Such riding is not comfortable, and it made me nervous. A puncture is one thing, but a blowout would be a ride-stopper.

We had another problem crop up en route to McEwen, one that could have been much more serious than it was. Near the top of a slight rise, I

*Chapter 11   Dickson to Camden*

noticed some shattered glass in the roadway ahead.  Normally I would ease out into the traffic lane to avoid such a hazard.  But traffic was fairly heavy on this stretch of US 70, and a motorist was unintentionally timing his arrival to the broken glass to coincide exactly with mine.  While I did not want to suffer yet another flat, I had no choice but to ride right over the glassy mess.  Fortunately my tires stood up to the test.

Josh was not so fortunate.  His tires suffered no damage, but just as he reached the field of glass, a large delivery truck passed him at high speed.  The truck's tires hit some of the glass in the travel lane, shooting a few shards at Josh.  The shard that hit his arm did not even break the skin, but the one that hit the side of his knee left a jagged-looking cut.  It could have been much worse:  a band-aid and Neosporin patched him up.  Josh pedaled and I bumped on into McEwen.

McEwen is a town of 1700 residents located in Humphreys County.  It comprises 1.9 square miles of scattered houses and businesses.  McEwen boasts the world's largest annual outdoor barbecue every July, the Irish Picnic.  More importantly to Josh and me, McEwen was where the hills would magically flatten out, or so we were told.   As we entered about mid-morning, our first order of business was to find a drug store.  Josh needed fresh band-aids.  He also needed an ace bandage for his right knee.  Injured two years previously, that knee was beginning to make its presence known.  Despite his wounds, Josh was performing quite well with the ride that day, handling the hills like a pro.  Surely McEwen would have a drug store.  But I held out no hope of a bicycle shop in a town so small.

Then I saw it:  the solution to my tire problem, right there across the highway!  It was so obvious--why hadn't I thought of it sooner?  "It" was Abernathy's Tire and Auto Repair.  Alright, so their specialty was car and truck tires, but just maybe. . . . I sent Josh on ahead in search of his bandages while I approached a big thirty-something good ole boy about my tire troubles.  His name was Billy.  (I've always wondered why average timid Williams like me go by "Bill" and big tough Williams like this guy prefer "Billy.")

*A Slice of Tennessee*

Billy was friendly and helpful. In no time his boss David had my bike up on a rack rubbing the rear tire with grease. The tire just wasn't seated properly, he explained, and the tube inside was caught in a bind. While he was working on it, a number of fire trucks raced by. Moments later David received a call with the local news: the pizza restaurant owner's house had burned down and the surrounding woods caught fire. People think of small towns as dull, but they have their share of drama. I sympathized with a man I'd never met who'd just lost his home to fire.

Within a few minutes the tire yielded, the flat spot popped out, and David aired it up full. Suddenly I was even more pumped up than the tire! My bump problem was solved!

**David Abernathy saved the ride that day!**

David wouldn't let me pay him anything. He and Billy seemed interested in my cross-state ride. Billy was raised in Humphreys County, so I told him of

*Chapter 11    Dickson to Camden*

my roots (way back) in Humphreys County.  My great-grandfather William ("Pa") Horner was a lifelong resident, having been born in the region to John Valentine Horner and his wife Elizabeth Dillworth Patterson.  Pa married Amanda Frances Pace and for many decades worked his farm and practiced medicine, often making house calls on horseback.  Billy listened politely, then said something that made my day and put the ride back into perspective.  "I've heard of him."  Having been raised in several locales in two different states, this stranger's acknowledgement of my heritage—even in this small degree—gave me chill bumps.  This ride was about rediscovering the Tennessee I've known most of my life and reconnecting with roots I'd almost forgotten.  But it was also about new friends.  So I thanked David and Billy profusely and set out on a much smoother ride.

Josh had found his bandages and rejoined me.  I was eager to get started again toward Waverly and another Billy I'd never met before, who also knew of my great-grandfather—primarily because Pa Horner was *his* great-grandfather also.

"Welcome to Waverly.  Character Counts in Tiger Country!" proclaimed the sign ushering us into town.  (The only tigers indigenous to the area are found at Waverly Central High School athletic events.)  The area was relatively flat, a nice change from the hills of the day before.  There are low ridges, however, to the north and south of town, the western fringes of the Highland Rim of Middle Tennessee.  Barely ten miles to the west stands the dividing line between the Middle and West grand divisions of the state:  the Tennessee River.

*A Slice of Tennessee*

**I hadn't been to Waverly since I was seven**

The name Waverly hails back to the popular author of the early 1800's, Sir Walter Scott and his Waverley novels. With its strong Confederate leanings during the Civil War and its connection with the notorious Jesse James (he once owned a farm nearby), this charming town of about 4000 has a colorful history. Among Waverly's more prominent residents are the late country songwriter and singer George Morgan and his equally talented daughter Lorrie. George was my father's first cousin.

This trip was my first to Waverly since I was seven years old, Josh's first ever. Josh seemed to like Waverly. Perhaps it was the satisfaction of reaching his destination. Perhaps it was the anticipation of finding roots of his own. We settled for a quick sandwich at the local Sonic drive-in (I guess for us it was a pedal-in). Then we called Billy Tucker.

*Chapter 11   Dickson to Camden*

Billy Tucker is a second cousin I had never met before.  Dad had told me a few weeks earlier about Billy, and I had talked with Billy by phone at that time. He was more than willing to meet us on our arrival to town and show us some of our heritage.  Billy was a lean, tanned outdoors-type with thinning hair (O.K., so he *doesn't* fit my previous assessment of "Billys").  In his seventy-six years he had worked hard both as a surveyor for the Tennessee Department of Transportation and a businessman managing his properties in the area.  His father Roscoe and my father were first cousins.

My late grandmother Mimi had often spoken of Roscoe.  His parents both died quite young, and Ma and Pa Horner (his grandparents) raised him. Dad's father Bill (my lands! there are a lot of Williams in Humphreys County Tennessee) had once gone out coon hunting on a cold moonlit night.  Roscoe, still just a young boy, begged to go along with the nearly-grown Bill.  Bill relented.  As Roscoe put on one of Bill's old coats with long tails, Bill called the hound dog, and off they went into the night.  Before long they scared up a coon. No one knows quite how it happened, but the coon caught Roscoe's coattails in his teeth and wouldn't let go.  Roscoe, terrified, started running in circles trying to shake it loose.  The hound dog was chasing after them both trying his best to get the coon.  Around and around they went.  Bill sat down in the midst of the ruckus and just laughed till he cried.

Billy showed up in no time, eager to take us wherever we wanted to go. The folks at Sonic gave us permission to lock up our bikes behind their store, and we set out.  Our first stop was Pa Horner's old home place.  All that remained of the original farm was a cleared site on Clydeton Road backing up to Kentucky Lake.  The lake was formed in 1944 by a TVA dam, and along with Lake Barkley on the Cumberland River, encloses Land Between the Lakes National Recreation Area.  With a canal connecting the two lakes, Land Between the Lakes is the largest inland peninsula in the United States.  The new lake inundated lands and homes, including the community of Birmingham, Tennessee, as well as most of my ancestor's farm.  I had not seen this site since 1960; not much was left there now.  When Dad showed us the spot decades ago, there was an old apple tree a few dozen yards from the road. That tree, he informed us, once stood just outside the back door of the farmhouse. Now even the tree was gone.

**Billy and I standing on Ma and Pa Horner's front porch**

But Billy's memory was intact. He easily stepped off the locations of the front porch, back porch, and Dr. Horner's eight by twelve foot office, where he often saw patients. As he fondly recalled his visits to the house, I could almost imagine it still there. Ma Horner, he informed us, remembered well the Civil War and often told stories from that conflict. She particularly remembered the Yankees coming through and confiscating all their chickens. Pa Horner was drafted to fight in the Confederate Army, but the war ended before he had to report. His father John did fight, serving under Nathan Bedford Forrest.

Ma and Pa raised eight children on that farm. And he didn't see all his patients in his office there. He also made house calls on horseback. One winter

*Chapter 11   Dickson to Camden*

night on a late call, after fording streams to reach a house, Pa required assistance to chop ice out of the stirrups so he could dismount. For such dedication Pa was often paid in chickens and vegetables.

Billy told me a Pa Horner story I'd never heard before: On one particularly difficult case he asked a respected doctor in town, Dr. Slayton, to make a house call with him. After attending the patient, they each presented the man with a bill for services. Dr. Slayton's bill was $4.00; Pa Horner's was $2.00. "Why," asked a puzzled Dr. Slayton, "did you charge him so little?" "You don't know that man like I do," Pa replied. "He'll never pay a dime to either of us. So you're out $4.00, and I'm only out $2.00!"

I responded to Billy with a Pa Horner story *he'd* never heard before. In 1936 Pa's son Bill (my grandfather) received a long distance call from his brother Jesse. Long distance calls back then were expensive and unreliable, so Bill knew the matter must be important. "Pa died," he heard his brother say. "Can you come on down here?" Bill assured him he'd leave Nashville immediately. What did he think about during the (then) long drive to Waverly? It was so unexpected—Pa was elderly but had been in good health. Ma was in frail health. How would the loss hit her? When Bill finally arrived to the spot on which Billy, Josh, and I now stood, a small group assembled on the front porch to meet him. But Bill stood and watched them in utter shock. For there in the midst of the group was the "deceased" Pa! Fortunately Jesse saw Bill's face and immediately discerned his confusion. Pulling his brother aside, Jesse explained that Bill had misunderstood him over the poor phone connection—it was *Ma* who had died. They never told Pa about the mix-up. Pa lived another eight years, still practicing medicine most of that time. He died at ninety-six, his county's oldest resident and his state's oldest physician.

Billy also affirmed other stories I'd heard about relatives in years gone by, such as Zack Morgan's encounter with a train. Zack was George's father. While walking across a railroad track in the woods as a young man, his foot caught under one of the rails. Before he could free it, a train came along. Zack's only option for survival was to lean as far off the track as he could. The

*A Slice of Tennessee*

train crushed his foot and ankle. He had to walk with a prosthetic foot the rest of his life.

Leaving the old home place, we proceeded on down to the end of Clydeton Road, the site of a number of cottages on the lake. Uncle Jesse and his friend Carl Meadows were once partners in this development, called Clydeton Docks. One small red brick house looked remarkably the same as it did fifty years earlier. In 1960 Mimi brought my sister Joyce and me up here to spend the summer. We stayed in this cottage, which sat on a hill overlooking the lake. During the mornings Mimi would take us to a local pool for swimming lessons. In the afternoon we often visited relatives and friends. Uncle Jesse himself had a house here. One night he had us over for a memorable fried catfish dinner.

As we started back up Clydeton Road, I looked around for the swimming pool, but it was nowhere in sight. Pointing across the road to a house with a particularly level front yard, Billy said, "That was the pool over there. They filled it in years ago." So nothing stays the same forever. But I was grateful for numerous reminders of a happy summer spent here in my childhood.

Before dropping us off Billy drove us by his own house and farm and then by an almost hidden graveyard containing the graves of Ma and Pa Horner and other relatives. All in all it was a wonderful afternoon for one who has lived many places, now rediscovering his ancestral roots.

Marcia and her mother caught up with us in Waverly. I enjoyed introducing them to the cousin I myself had met only that afternoon. Josh loaded his bike into their vehicle. Having reached his goal of Waverly, he was done biking for awhile. I would pedal another twenty miles to Camden and meet them there for dinner. But I would miss my excellent riding companion of the previous two days. I will always be grateful that he took the time to ride with his Dad.

Pa Horner gave his seven children roots. A strict Primitive Baptist, he sought to instill a love for God and proper values. Several of his children

Chapter 11   Dickson to Camden

remained in Waverly all their lives.  Pa was wise enough, however, to give his eight children wings also.  He allowed them to use opportunities to develop their potential, even if it meant their moving away.  Among his progeny over the generations would be country music performers, a Washington lobbyist for the U.S. Post Office, businessmen, farmers, technicians, a T.D.O.T. surveyor, and even a preacher.  The behavior of some of his descendants, I'm sure, was disappointing at times.  But the blessings in giving his children wings far outweighed the risk.

**I sure wish I could have known them**

The terrain was much flatter west of town, but now I faced a significant headwind, the first ominous sign of thunderstorms moving into the region.

123

Would I be able to ride on another two days? Or would the weather foul up my plans?

In less than an hour I passed another milestone. I was not just crossing the Tennessee River/Kentucky Lake. Having traversed two grand divisions of the state by bicycle, I was now entering the third: West Tennessee. The long reinforced concrete structure afforded excellent views of the lake in both directions. An older steel truss railroad bridge ran parallel to the highway bridge. The steam generation plant at New Johnsonville was visible on the eastern shore of the river. Completed in 1952, it is the oldest such plant in the TVA system, but its ten coal-fired units maintain an excellent record of efficiency, generating enough electricity to supply 400,000 homes. The wind gusting across the traffic lanes was terrific; I had to lean against the railing as I snapped pictures to avoid losing my footing.

**Kentucky Lake: The ancestral home of my dinner that night?**

I rode on into Camden, pondering the blessings I'd experienced that day, reconnecting with my roots while simultaneously enjoying my wings.

I rejoined Marcia and Josh at The Catfish Place in Camden for dinner. The waitress brought us out plates piled high with more catfish fillets and hush puppies than I'd ever seen assembled in one place. And those cats died for a worthy cause! Our meal consisted of local pond-raised, grain-fed catfish. (They taste a little milder than river catfish and are served boneless.) But I'm sure

*Chapter 11   Dickson to Camden*

their ancestors came out of the Tennessee River some generations back. So even these catfish had roots. But apparently they also had wings—which ultimately landed them onto our plates. Roots and wings—what a blessing!

**Those catfish died for a worthy cause**

*A Slice of Tennessee*

**55.30 miles for the day**

**396.02 miles total**

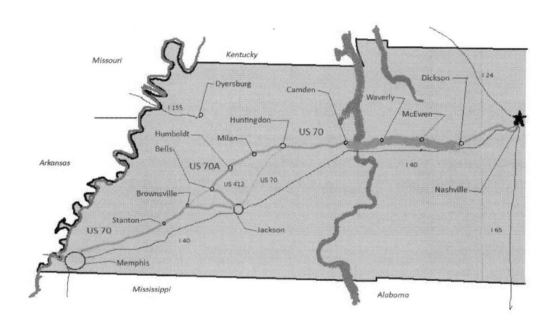

# Chapter 12  Camden to Jackson
## Agriculture & Commerce

   I knew it was too good to last: two days of beautiful spring weather with partly sunny skies and warm temperatures—and a riding partner that would please any dad—my son Josh.

   An hour earlier Josh, Marcia, her mother, and I had been happily doing our part to support the local economy (channel catfish is the official state commercial fish) at a Camden institution, The Catfish Place. Still operating on a cash-only basis, this unassuming establishment had been making palates happy for decades. Our meal was indeed memorable, but now the others had gone home.

*A Slice of Tennessee*

And the clouds were rolling in as the foul weather finally seemed to be catching up to us. Over dinner Josh had employed his ubiquitous Blackberry to obtain a weather forecast: thunderstorms through the night, rain possibly continuing until noon on Wednesday. It was that word *possibly* that disturbed me. If it were seventy percent or more chance of rain, I could honorably end my riding for this trip and return to Nashville with Marcia and Josh. If it were only a slight chance of rain, I could continue my ride in confidence. But with an almost even chance, I'd either have to dig out my clunky rain poncho and prepare for a wet ride OR chicken out on the ride and maybe live to regret the wasted opportunity. In the end the words *wasted opportunity* disturbed me far more than the word *possibly*. So I bid the others farewell and secured a room for the night.

Hence, I was alone again. Solitude is an odd commodity. We often desire it. But when we obtain it, we wish down inside we weren't so alone. The solitude of riding the highway, making my own decisions on stops and speed and destinations was downright therapeutic. I am reminded here of Gordon Lightfoot's song "Carefree Highway." Yet it sure was good at times to have a riding partner, someone to talk to, someone with whom to share the wonder of the ride and each new discovery. Josh had filled that role well for two days. Barry Chamberlain would fill it from Jackson to Memphis. Meanwhile I was on my own again. Maybe it wouldn't be bad. There were always new people to meet on the ride.

And was I really on my own? The Best Western Homeplace Inn in Camden not only served up a clean comfortable room and a hot breakfast. They also provided each room with a Gideon Bible and a Daily Bread devotional book. Wednesday's lesson was from Acts 18:7-11—despite opposition the Apostle Paul had encountered along the way, God assured him that there in Corinth he could speak freely for Christ without attack for months to come. The operative words were, *"For I am with you."* It was a good reminder that He'd be with me that day, too.

128

*Chapter 12   Camden to Jackson*

And why was I so worried about rain, anyway?  Didn't I start this ride in the rain last fall near Newport?  Yes.  And didn't I thoroughly enjoy beginning this fabulous adventure, even in the rain?  Yes.  And were my soggy wet clothes really that uncomfortable that first day of riding?  Yes. (Oh well, two out of three ain't bad.)  But rain is part of the fabric of Tennessee as surely as colorful leaves, historical sites, and tasty catfish.  Indeed it plays a major part in the culture of agriculture so prominent in West Tennessee.  *Agriculture and Commerce*—that is the Tennessee state motto.  On this part of my ride I would experience the overlap of both as I rode through several small towns whose livelihood depended largely on the produce of the surrounding farms.

I took the luxury of sleeping in late the next morning.  Not only was I tired from two days of riding, but I also wanted to give the rain that had been falling all night a chance to dissipate.  Loading up on bacon, eggs, biscuits, and gravy at the Best Western, I prepared to meet the rain head-on about 9:00am.  But to my utter amazement the clouds showed signs of breaking up as I started out.  The rain had slowed to a mere mist.  I donned the poncho, tying my backpack straps around my waist to keep the plastic from billowing up around me as I rode, and took off.  This wasn't so bad.  Lon Chenowith, my good preacher buddy and inspiration for this trip, had hiked many a day along the Appalachian Trail in heavy downpours and even in knee-deep snow.  I had it easy.

My pedaling soon took me within three miles of the site of the plane crash that killed Patsy cline.  What a rich, expressive voice she had.  In the mid-1950's she won an Arthur Godfrey Talent Scouts contest on television (the early equivalent of American idol).  By 1960 she was singing with the Grand Ole Opry.  She would win numerous awards for hits such as "Crazy" and "I Fall to Pieces."

Barely two years prior to the plane crash, a Nashville traffic accident had nearly ended Patsy's life.  Out of that trial came months of hospitalization and

*A Slice of Tennessee*

rehabilitation—but also a return to her career. She came back a changed woman with a strong recommitment to Christ.

But at dawn on March 6, 1963, local rescuers found the wreckage of the yellow plane that carried Patsy along with entertainers Cowboy Copas, Hawkshaw Hawkins, and Randy Hughes. All were killed. Country music fans were devastated. Passing near the site of this tragedy took my mind off the misty cool weather.


Bruceton was the first of numerous tiny towns I would traverse on my ride this particular day. It looked like a ghost town. I don't recall seeing anyone there, just an occasional passing car. One of those temporary advertising signs in a parking lot in front of a boarded up building seemed to sum up the local mood: "Where the ____'s my bailout?" Maybe the next town would be a little more inviting. Hollow Rock. Yes, now I was definitely in Carroll County. Believe it or not, I had been to Hollow Rock before, actually knew a resident there. She was a fellow freshman at the University of Tennessee at Martin back in 1972, a girl named Pat. My roommate John Claxton was fortunate enough to have wheels, a 1966 Chevy II. One weekend he had given me, Pat from Hollow Rock, Debbie from MacKenzie, and Linda from somewhere, a ride to Nashville, where they attended a Christian conference. I attended to my then girlfriend and now wife Marcia, who was finishing high school that year. On the way back to campus Sunday evening, Pat talked John into swinging by her house for a few minutes, where we visited with her mother. Pat told us this town that presently boasts 963 residents was named by an explorer who discovered a hollow rock nearby. Hence, my introduction to the town through which I was now pedaling. A cute little community, it didn't appear to have changed much in thirty-seven years.

Soon the houses and businesses of a larger town came into view. Huntingdon was the last town I'd see before I began to pass the large open fields of West Tennessee. Huntingdon boasts about 4300 residents. John and I

Chapter 12   Camden to Jackson

knew a UTM upper classman named Bobby Tucker from here.  He called the city "the capital of Carroll County."  I guess it is—the county courthouse is located there.  I stopped at a bank off the courthouse square looking for a familiar ATM that wouldn't charge me a user fee.   I was down to $8.00 cash, and small towns still run largely on cash, not plastic.  A friendly teller informed me that my bank didn't have a machine in the area.  However, she was impressed with my bike ride and suggested nearby Mallard's restaurant for lunch.  Instead, I pedaled on out toward WalMart, where I could buy some cheap needed item with my debit card and get cash out for free.  Stopping on the way at CB's Barbecue, I enjoyed a pork plate, which left me a dollar to spare.  A few minutes later I found WalMart, bought a cheap tire gauge, and obtained my needed cash.

**The Capital of Carroll County**

I hardly recognized anything in Huntingdon from my UTM days passing through here.  However, I recalled another student, Debbie Cannon, who made her home in this town.  She had survived the devastating tornado that ripped through the area in 1970.  Debbie, who had a strong faith in the Lord, had calmly gone through the house opening windows (as experts suggested in those

*A Slice of Tennessee*

days) as the funnel cloud was approaching. The Lord spared her and her family's house. Debbie once told me that the town was named for a carving a hunter left on a nearby tree, "Hunting done."

Huntingdon brought me to another decision point: US 70 splits into 70 going to Jackson and Brownsville and 70A going to Milan, Humboldt, Bells, then Brownsville. I wanted to explore *both* routes and see all the Tennessee I could. So I hit on a compromise: 70A to Humboldt, lodge there for the night, and then on back to Jackson on a different highway. Next time I could ride Jackson to Memphis on 70. Not exactly US 70 all the way, but hey! it's *my* ride, isn't it? Oh, the freedom of starting out *here* and going *somewhere* before day's end.

The rain was long gone by now. But everywhere I looked around me I could see the fruits of its labor: fields with lush green wheat (it turns golden-amber by June) or the remains of last year's cotton or corn crops. When I was a young college student, West Tennessee had struck me as bland and unattractive. But bicycle speed improves one's perspective. I was riding through some of the richest farm land in the country. And those open fields and big sky were frequently punctuated by patches of woods and the cute little houses of hard-working families who made their living off this land.

The highway itself was not the best I'd ever pedaled over. The shoulder, when present at all, was composed of fifteen inches of rumble strip, designed to keep vehicles from straying off the road. Personally I resented this design by the same Department of Transportation I once worked for, which favored the safety of numerous cars and eighteen-wheelers on this route over the comfort of the occasional bicyclist like me. Where were their priorities? At least the motorists were courteous for the most part and seemed to know how to drive around bicycles. The traffic was occasionally distracting but not frightening, even as big trucks zipped around me.

The road between Atwood and Milan revealed that the term *agriculture* takes in more than just crops. It also includes the raising of livestock. I saw a variety of animals in the fields along this stretch of highway, including goats,

*Chapter 12    Camden to Jackson*

mules, donkeys, cattle, and horses.  Rounding one bend, I came upon fifteen large black bulls lying in the grass next to the fence, barely ten feet off the road.  Another bull was standing, facing them as if he were giving them a lecture on cleanliness or proper grazing etiquette.  As I pulled up to snap a quick picture of this bovine conclave, I apparently spooked the principals involved, and the cattle conference dispersed.  Further down the highway I passed a field full of spotted, speckled, and mottled goats.  I wondered if they were descended from Jacob's flock (see Genesis 30:25-43).  And how does one differentiate between a *donkey* and a *mule*?  I really don't know, but if you take your best guess and identify them with confidence, probably no one will challenge you (they don't know either).

**I didn't mean to break up the meeting**

Outside of Milan I made another one of those serendipitous discoveries: the West Tennessee Agricultural Museum on the site of the University of Tennessee's Research and Education Center at Milan. The museum proudly showcased the agricultural products of the area, cotton being prominent among them. Twenty-three counties in Tennessee produce cotton, most of them in the western end of the state. Over half a million acres are devoted to cotton every year with each acre producing 600 to 900 pounds. What intrigued me, however, was the wide variety of products made from cotton. In addition to the obvious, such as denim, terry cloth, chambray, and corduroy, cotton makes its appearance in coffee filters, gun powder, paper, and bookbinding as well. And cottonseed oil is used in mayonnaise, salad dressing, cooking oil, and many processed foods.

**No-Till is to tractors as tractors were to those horse-drawn plows**

The museum also had displays commemorating the hard life of early settlers in Tennessee as they cleared and cultivated the land. One display, however, revealed the more recent pioneering efforts on this very site by Tom McCutcheon relative to conservation tillage.

Tennessee is blessed with good, rich, fertile soils in many parts of the state. Unfortunately, these soils are often highly erodible, a major problem for farmers. But the tireless research efforts of McCutcheon and others developed

*Chapter 12    Camden to Jackson*

the agricultural process called No-Till.  This method allows planting in narrow slots or small drilled holes without extensive tilling of a field, both cutting down erosion by sixty percent and dramatically reducing production costs.  No-Till is now the preferred method of tillage by most Tennessee farmers and is appearing in many other countries as well.  Since 1981 Milan has hosted the biennial Milan No-Till Field Day to highlight the latest innovations in this agricultural method.

The curator of the museum was quite helpful in explaining the displays.  She also suggested a place for lodging once I made Humboldt.  And we had some past experience in common—she had studied at UTM about the same time I was there.  I asked if she knew Debbie Cannon from Huntingdon.  *"Dr. Debbie Cannon,"* she corrected me, had earned her doctorate in home economics and done quite well.  I was not surprised.

Was West Tennessee not as flat as I remembered?  Or were even mild upgrades wearing on me after nearly three days of pedaling?  I don't know which, but I was sure glad to see Humboldt come into view.  I knew very little about the town.  Another former UTM acquaintance, who went by the moniker Chickee, had called Humboldt home.  And a sign on the outskirts informed visitors that Doug Atkins is a native son.  Atkins played football for the University of Tennessee in the early 1950's, was personally recruited by Coach General Robert Neyland, and went on to play pro for the Browns, the Bears, and the Saints.  He was inducted into both the College Football and Pro Football Halls of Fame.  Any connection to my Big Orange alma mater was a good sign.

Despite those glowing attributes, I still had some trepidation upon entering the city.  One store clerk I had met a few miles back had warned me not to ride my bike through the city—one side of town was pretty rough.  Not wanting to get shot this trip, I planned to lodge out on the bypass, then bypass the downtown on my way to Jackson the next morning.  But spying a decent-looking mom and pop motel, I opted for a second opinion on the lodging.  At a major intersection a car full of twenty-somethings stopped at a red light.  A young man yelled and pointed, asking what was that strange-looking stick protruding from my helmet. Taking optimum advantage of the quickly waning red light, I hastily replied, "My rear-view mirror. Do you know Humboldt? Where's a good place to stay the night?" As the light greened up, he pointed across the highway and shouted, "That's as good a place as any." He waved as the car sped on. Who could argue with such a sterling recommendation? I stayed the night there. It was clean. I think they'd even washed the sheets.

**Even the water tower proudly proclaims agriculture**

**54.59 miles for the day**

**450.61miles total**

The next morning early I did a brave thing: ignoring the store clerk's warning, I pedaled on into downtown Humboldt—right through the rough part of town—and lived to tell about it. Actually, I've ridden my bike through worse

## Chapter 12   Camden to Jackson

areas. Why let one individual spook me? This was my opportunity to see Humboldt firsthand. This quaint town of nearly 10,000 residents has annually hosted the West Tennessee Strawberry Festival since 1934 and boasts of a museum of art, a division of ConAgra Foods, and of course, a commercial cotton gin.

As I entered the downtown area, my feet exerted their independent will and pedaled right past Highway US 45 to Jackson. Their message soon reached my brain. Why not pedal on to Bells, *then* back to Jackson? Marcia had agreed to meet me in Jackson because I could not arrange a one-way car rental from there. But since she would not arrive in Jackson till almost noon, I had plenty of time, and I'd never been to Bells. Oh, the joy of starting out *here* and pedaling *somewhere*.

**I definitely had a glow about me that morning**

What a morning for a ride. This was one of the prettiest stretches I'd seen in West Tennessee—mild hills, groves of trees, and of course open fields, similar to what I had ridden through the day before but somehow more picturesque. The early morning sun threw my shadow off into the adjacent pasture as I pedaled by. A yellow halo encircled the shadow. I snapped a quick picture as I rode (in between passing eighteen wheelers) and continued on to Bells.

**Even little Bells gets in on the agriculture action**

A charming little town of 2171 residents, Bells was founded by John and William Bell, who in the early 1800's bought up land at a dollar an acre. Originally called Bells Depot and located in Haywood County, the name was changed to Bells and the town annexed into Crockett County in 1887. Bells sports a homey downtown with a diner, bank, scattered stores, attractive homes, and one of the largest frozen vegetable suppliers in the United States, the PictSweet Company, specializing in blackeyed peas, okra, sweet corn, carrots, and other local commodities. An annual highlight of this city is the West Tennessee Okra Festival, which features a horse show, beauty pageant, street carnival, and other activities. *Everything* in this end of the state seems

*Chapter 12   Camden to Jackson*

tied to agriculture. A nearby state historical marker even informs that large-scale strawberry growing in Tennessee was brought into the state by David Brandenburg of Maryland in 1867.

It was time to depart US 70A for Highway 412 and the twelve miles back to Jackson, where I would link up once more with US 70. But where was 412? You'd think in a town the size of Bells, the major roads would be obvious. But 412 was not. So I swallowed my manly pride and asked a citizen on the sidewalk how to get there. Following his instructions, I quickly discovered, would send me in the wrong direction. I figured out the correct route on my own. It still amazes me how little some locals know about their own town.

**Jackson is proud of its Rock-A-Billy Connections**

Finally I was on my way to Jackson, which, I would learn from a mural covering the side of an old brick building, was the birthplace of the Rockabilly sound popularized by Johnny Cash. But the only noteworthy sight en route there along the interstate-like Highway 412 was the old house with a junked vehicle in the front yard—not the usual car or truck but a Toyota Celica-turned-helicopter. I have no idea the story behind that out-of-service rustbucket, but I wouldn't be surprised if it had something to do with agriculture.

*Agriculture* (cotton and cattle, corn and soybeans, tobacco and wheat) *and Commerce* (PictSweet, ConAgra, Farmers Gin of Humboldt)—an appropriate motto for the state I was pedaling through.

**A Toyota Celicopter?**

*Chapter 12  Camden to Jackson*

**39.09 miles for the day**

**489.70miles total**

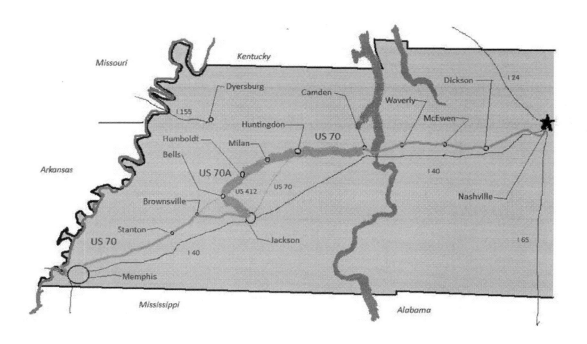

*A Slice of Tennessee*

# Chapter 13  Jackson to Memphis:  Part I
## Southern Tradition

It began as a wispy dream at the North Carolina state line and suddenly took on a life of its own.  Now here I was approaching the finish line.  I was already homesick for the ride and it wasn't even over yet.  Exploring the state I love by bicycle down yesteryear's main street (Highway US 70) had been somewhat akin to reading a good mystery novel:  as the finish grew closer, I had the mad desire to reach the conclusion; yet, I did not want the experience to end.  Indeed, I have come to realize that the destination is not the purpose of the trip.  The journey itself *is* the destination.

This ride being so far to the west, the logistics were more of a challenge than ever.  My old high school buddy Barry Chamberlain from Houston would make the two-day ride with me from Jackson to the finish line.  Getting to the starting point was no problem. I met Barry at his parents' house in Nashville on Sunday evening, June 28, and we drove to Jackson to lodge for the night.

**Barry would prove another worthy riding partner**

But neither Marcia nor Barry's wife Mona was available to drive the chase car and bring us back from Memphis. An appeal to southern hospitality solved the front end of our problem: a place to park my vehicle in Jackson. Drawing on my credentials as a Baptist minister, I found a local Baptist church in Jackson via the internet and contacted the staff. Brian Wimberley of Poplar Heights Baptist Church was most gracious. He arranged for us to park my minivan at their church parsonage for safe-keeping while we pedaled to Memphis. Brian's name sounded familiar. "When I was a freshman at the University of Tennessee at Martin in 1971, I shared a dorm suite with a Mike

## Chapter 13   Jackson to Memphis: Part I

Wimberley from Paris, Tennessee," I told him.  "Mike's my uncle," said Brian.  The more I've ridden across this state, the smaller it has become.

Memories almost four decades old began to flood in.  John Claxton and I shared a dorm room.  We were high school buddies from Nashville.  Mike from Paris and Keith from Waverly shared the adjoining room in our suite.  A bathroom connected the rooms.  Mike was constantly coming into our room, standing and gazing out our window (he liked our view better than his), and muttering, "Well, here we are, college men."  Mike had a nice bicycle.  And he was proud of it!  He was mad as a hornet the weekend Benny Edwards and I secretly deflated the tires.  Back then I thought it was funny.  Now I can sympathize with Mike.  Don't touch my bike!

Another appeal to southern hospitality was necessary to solve the back end of our problem:  returning from Memphis to our vehicle in Jackson at the conclusion of our ride.  This time the solution came in the form of a Baptist Collegiate Ministry staffer.  The director himself, Jeff Miller, agreed to drive us back to Jackson.  (I promised him dinner as part of the arrangement.)

One problem proved more troublesome.  The lodging options between Jackson and Memphis along US 70 were quite limited.  Nothing seemed to be available anywhere near the half-way point of our ride.  Finally, I located a small motel via the internet near Stanton that looked suitable.  We were ready to ride!

Southern hospitality is still very much alive in Tennessee.  Barry and I would encounter it frequently in our two days on the road.  It's a southern tradition.  And this end of the state holds on to traditions fiercely.  There is a large sign, for instance, on a farm near Brownsville proudly proclaiming, "100% Pure Estate Bottled Sweet Sorghum—Preserving a Southern Tradition."

*A Slice of Tennessee*

**A right flavorful southern tradition**

Sweet Sorghum is indeed sweet. It is a delightful addition to homemade buttermilk biscuits, another southern tradition. Making sorghum is a labor-intensive process that involves crushing the sorghum cane stalks and cooking and stirring the juice for over two hours. Twenty gallons of juice cooks down to just two gallons of dark amber syrup. Slave labor was replaced with paid labor after the War Between the States. After World War II even paid farm laborers became increasingly scarce. So the twenty million gallons previously produced annually has dwindled down to just one million. But it's good to know that someone is preserving this southern tradition. Discovering such traditions and watching local folks preserve them would make this ride an interesting one.

We began our ride early Monday morning. Parking our minivan at the Poplar Heights Church parsonage, we unloaded our bikes and strapped on our helmets. It felt odd looking at the vehicle and realizing we would not ride in it again before pedaling to Memphis, crossing the Old Bridge over the Mississippi River, and catching a ride back—*if* everything went according to plan. But the bright sunny 68 degree morning (on its way up to 91 degrees) boosted our confidence. I was wearing my fluorescent yellow *Wallace Hydroseeding* T-shirt

Chapter 13   Jackson to Memphis: Part I

for the occasion.  Matt Wallace, the deacon who gave me the Diamondback Crestview that I rode halfway across Tennessee, was a schoolteacher in Maryland who had a summer hydroseeding business.  It seemed fitting to honor this man who had contributed so importantly to the Ride.

Before we could depart, Wes Franklin came out of his house to greet us.  A personable man, Wes lived in the parsonage and ministered to students at Union University nearby.  He was only too happy to share his driveway with two ambitious bikers--our first sampling of the southern tradition of hospitality that day.

**New friends like Wes made the ride possible**

We had not pedaled far before experiencing our second taste of southern hospitality that morning. As we stopped at a convenience store for a Gatorade fill-up, a man named Jerry greeted us in the parking lot. Dressed in old worn work clothes and pushing an old well-used bicycle, Jerry showed an immediate interest in our bikes. He had ridden his a half mile from home to the store. And being a bike rider himself, Jerry was intrigued by our ride to Memphis. As we started off again, he stopped us and asked, "Can I ride with you as far as my house?" So we had another partner in the ride, for at least the next half mile, after which Jerry peeled off and bade us goodbye.

**One of three riding partners on my statewide ride**

*Chapter 13   Jackson to Memphis: Part I*

More hospitality awaited us further down the road in Brownsville. This town of about 11,000 was named for Jacob Jennings Brown, who served as an officer in the War of 1812, the war in which Tennessee derived her fame as "The Volunteer State" (and yes, the nickname really does pre-date University of Tennessee football). Brownsville is the only built-up area of any size between Jackson and Memphis. The day was rapidly growing warmer, and we stopped to rest in the shade on the lawn of the (traditional) courthouse square. Barry made himself at home lying down on the grass. Soon I noticed a smartly dressed older man speaking with him. Oh no, I thought, he thinks Barry's a vagrant. But their subsequent laughter eased my mind and puzzled it simultaneously. It seems that a foreclosure sale slated for the courthouse that morning had been cancelled. The kind gentleman simply wanted to make sure Barry wasn't waiting around for it. Barry replied, "No, but tell me what you've got—I might be interested." Mona would have loved that one—Barry rides with me and comes home with real estate in Brownsville.

**The Brownsville Courthouse shade felt good**

That might not have been such a bad deal after all. Brownsville looked like a good place to live. Claiborne Thornton, prominent in Tennessee

*A Slice of Tennessee*

homeschooling circles, was originally from here. I knew Claiborne from the Tennessee Department of Transportation in the late 1970's. He told me once that every summer in Brownsville, the Thornton family would have a week-long reunion. This grand event would feature food, fellowship, camping out, and daily preaching. They referred to it as "the camp meeting." What a way to celebrate family in the South!

Lunch in Brownsville revealed another West Tennessee tradition that the locals defended vigorously: pork barbecue. Backyard Barbecue proved to be no disappointment, with its pulled pork sandwiches, good cole slaw (always a test of a good barbecue restaurant), and classic movie posters adorning the walls. We were to find out however, that many such establishments compete for the customers, and every local can tell you which one is the best. Indeed, I had already been advised of several "best" barbecue restaurants in Memphis; however, my heart was set on the ribs at Rendezvous.

The deliciously cool morning had quickly turned into a hot afternoon. The stretch of US 70 west of Brownsville had little shoulder, but the traffic was light. Since the power lines ran along our side of the road, the few shady spots usually appeared on the other side. I couldn't resist stopping at a produce stand some young people were tending in front of their house. It wasn't the produce—it was the shade of the awning. Enzo and Robin were quite friendly and glad to share their shade with two weary bikers. But our first figurative dark cloud appeared on the horizon as they asked where we were staying that night. The motel in Stanton, I informed them. They scratched their heads wondering what this crazy biker was talking about. "There's *nothing* in Stanton," they informed us. We thanked them politely and rode on, knowing that the internet told us there *was* a motel there and the internet does not lie!

But as we arrived in this community of 615 people, we discovered to our chagrin that the locals know more about Haywood County than the internet does. We met a friendly young man named Carson at a convenience store (the

*Chapter 13   Jackson to Memphis: Part I*

only commercial establishment in town).  He knew our motel—it was seven miles off the highway near I-40, and there were no more motels on US 70 until Memphis.  And we weren't even to the halfway point of our two-day ride.  Staying at our intended motel would put a sixty-plus mile day ahead of us the next day, a doubtful goal in the increasing heat and humidity.  While we pondered our dilemma, Carson excitedly told us of the Justin Timberlake movie that was filmed in Stanton.

*Black Snake Moan* is a rough-edged version of the literary classic *Silas Marner* set in contemporary rural southern culture.  They picked the right place to film it, I thought.  Stanton was southern and certainly rural.  Nevertheless, Carson was proud of his little town.

Personally, I was less concerned about the cultural offerings of Stanton than I was about where we'd stop and sleep.  Where did Justin Timberlake sleep during the filming?  the motel at I-40?  Before the day was out, Barry and I might truly be vagrants.

**Definitely *not* the motel the internet told us about**

*A Slice of Tennessee*

We weren't entirely without options. The infallible internet had revealed a lodging establishment in nearby Galloway. Further research, however, determined that it was a nursing home. Barry and I were not strapping young men anymore, but we certainly were not ready for a stay at Terminal Towers Inn. I could see it clearly: "We'd like a room for the night with a view." "Yes, sir, would you prefer one with or without oxygen? And I'll need to see your Medicare card." But maybe they would feel sorry enough for us to allow us to doze in their lobby that night.

I did have one more drawing card: my internet searching had turned up a bed and breakfast somewhere in the area, Little Acorn Farm. But B & B's tend to be expensive. And they usually require advanced reservations. Typically they have only one bed per room (not an attractive option to two sweaty bikers). But we were desperate. I pulled out my cell phone. Inwardly I groaned—the phone displayed only one cell bar. How could the Hollywood movie people conduct all their movie business here on the strength of one cell bar? I held my breath and dialed the number I'd had the good sense to put in my billfold.

"Little Acorn Farm," responded a pleasant voice on the other end, remarkably strong for one cell bar. It was Jaynee Bodansky, who along with her husband Les ran the B & B.

"No, you don't need a reservation," she assured us, as I explained our situation. Their price for a room and a "farm fresh breakfast" the next morning was actually quite reasonable. So why did I hesitate?

"I'm trying to decide on one room or two. I think we'd each prefer to sleep solo after a long hot day riding," I confessed, without telling her that money is always tight for a poor preacher.

Jayne offered us two rooms at a considerably reduced rate. I ran it by Barry—it was a go. And the location, just a few miles down the road, would put

Chapter 13  Jackson to Memphis: Part I

us in a much better position for the next day's ride.  Jehovah Jireh—the Lord Provides!  And southern hospitality still prevails!

**Definitely a cut above the nearby nursing home**

B & B's don't serve dinner.  So we stopped at the one convenience store between Stanton and Mason and made ourselves sandwiches to go on their table in the back.  Then we pedaled two more miles out to Little Acorn Farm.  Those last two miles are always the longest and hardest.  But our oasis finally came into view.

Les met us outside and quickly introduced us to Jaynee.  They made us feel quite welcome in their home, more like houseguests than paying customers.  She escorted us to our rooms, each one equipped with its own bath, and left us to clean up.  That shower was heavenly!  An array of herbal soaps and shampoo enhanced the experience.

Soon Barry and I were sitting on the Bodansky's front porch, looking out over their farm, and enjoying our sandwiches.  Afterward we roamed over the back yard, admiring their giant checkerboard and the bronze plaque that declared "On this sight in 1897, nothing happened."  As dusk descended, Les proudly showed us his extensive blueberry bushes.  Jaynee went a step further, giving us each a bowl with orders to pick some.  Back inside the house, she topped our berries with generous portions of all natural vanilla ice cream.

**Les and Jaynee epitomized southern hospitality**

As we sat in their den savoring every bite of our rich dessert, the Bodanskys shared some of their background with us.  They are committed Christians.  Their son and his wife had previously moved to the Memphis area.  Les and Jaynee came down to visit, found the farm, and moved here with the dream of operating the B & B.  They had been here less than two years.

Well, their dream had proved a lifesaver to Barry and me that hot June evening.  We would sit up for another hour discussing the two topics acquaintances usually avoid:  religion and politics.  And then off to fantastically comfortable beds and a good night's sleep.

*Chapter 13   Jackson to Memphis: Part I*

**Little Acorn, Big Checkerboard**

   This sweet couple did as much as anyone we'd meet in our two days on the road to preserve the tradition of southern hospitality. That is significant since they had so recently moved to Tennessee from—*Canada* (Vancouver, B.C.).

   We had one more day of riding to reach my original destination of the state line / Mississippi River. Again I was reminded that the journey itself *is* the destination.

# A Slice of Tennessee

**54.75 miles for the day**

**544.45 miles total**

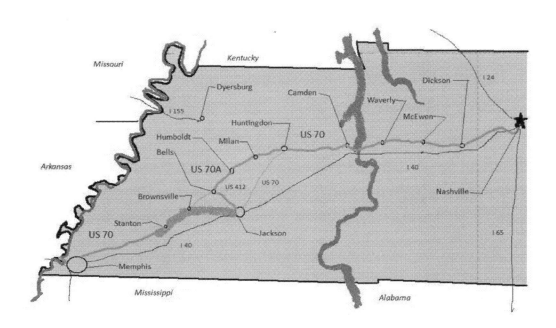

# Chapter 14  Jackson to Memphis:  Part II
## Southern Tradition

"Bed & Breakfast" implies not only a good night's rest but also a savory meal in the morning.  Little Acorn Farm did not disappoint on either front.  The advertised "farm fresh breakfast" truly was: egg and potato casserole, honeydew melon, apple sauce, sausage links, toast with jelly (on fancy bread, I might add), and orange juice.  Sitting beside each of our plates in the sunny dining room was a hat embroidered with "Little Acorn Farm" on the front and adorned with an "I Believe" button on the side.  I suspect the Bodanskys didn't give those to every guest.  It made us feel special.

*A Slice of Tennessee*

My T-shirt for the day was one Josh had given me a month earlier for my 56th birthday: emblazoned on the front was a picture of me and my bicycle posing next to the "Welcome to Waverly" sign. He had taken it in March when he accompanied me from Nashville to Waverly.

The day was sunshiny and warm. What a way to start the last day of the ride that began in the chilly rain near Newport last fall. Thanking the Bodanskys for their kindness, Barry and I set out, eager to encounter still more examples of carefully preserved southern tradition before day's end.

The first town down the road that morning was Galloway. We passed the infamous nursing home, grateful again for the night's lodging we'd found. In no time we were back out in the country again.

**The Monster that ate the South**

Stopping for a water break, Barry urged me to snap a picture of a pervasive if unintended southern tradition: kudzu. Sometimes called "mile a

Chapter 14   Jackson to Memphis: Part II

minute vine" or "the vine that ate the South," kudzu is a legume native to southern Japan.  It was first introduced into the United States in 1876 as a forage crop and an ornamental plant.  However, in the South the Civilian Conservation Corps planted it extensively for erosion control.  With ideal growing conditions and no natural predators, it quickly became an official nuisance weed.  It takes only a few weeks for this rapidly-growing vine to cover stone walls, trees, even old junked cars (by the way, another pervasive southern tradition).  After a few minutes Barry seemed impatient to get started again.  I don't think he liked the way the kudzu was looking at us.

**The Mississippi Embayment can be quite scenic**

*A Slice of Tennessee*

Soon we crossed the lazy, winding Loosahatchie River. Barry, always the geologist, noted that we were now in the Mississippi Embayment, part of the Mississippi Alluvial Plain. According to Wikipedia it is a northward continuation of the fluvial sediments of the Mississippi River Delta to its confluence with the Ohio River at Cairo, Illinois. (I don't know what that means, but it sounds impressive.) I have always been fascinated by the kinks and twists and course changes of the Mississippi River. Barry recommended I read *Rising Tide: The Great Mississippi Flood of 1927 and How It Changed America* by John M. Barry. (I suspected he liked it for the author's last name, but I put it on my list anyway.)

Not long after we entered Shelby County and Arlington, we encountered the built-up area that would continue unabated for the rest of the ride. It was good to see civilization again, but the day was quickly growing hotter and more humid than the day before. The terrain was surprisingly hilly (hey—I thought it was all downhill from Crossville). We still had much riding ahead of us. There was no way, however, I was going to let such trivialities keep me from finishing this ride. I was too close. I could almost taste it. I was confident Barry would make it to the finish line also. But if not, I'd note where he went down and phone the location to the paramedics. In the meantime, nothing could stop me. Nothing except a two-inch cotter pin lying in my path. I never saw it. I just heard the sickening *pop!* and felt the familiar *bump bump* of a flat tire.

We set to work immediately. My best tire-change time, from dismounting to pedaling off again (including installing the new tube *and* patching the old one) is just under fifteen minutes. We made good time here, too. I was not satisfied, however, with the patch in the old tube—the cotter pin had put a long tear into it. I wasn't sure the patch would hold, and there was still a lot of Memphis to pedal through. I'd be without a reliable spare. But I'd pedal on the rims to the River if I had to!

Memphis is familiar territory to Barry. He graduated from the University of Memphis (formerly Memphis State University) in the mid 1970's. He led us off US 70 for several blocks onto a parallel road to avoid the heaviest traffic.

*Chapter 14   Jackson to Memphis:  Part II*

We rejoined the highway again where it runs past Overton Park.  Talk about preserving southern tradition—the Park not only is home to cultural offerings ranging from an art school and museum to a sprawling zoo to a nine-hole golf course; in addition, this 342 acre enclosure in Midtown Memphis boasts one of the largest old-growth forests in any major metropolitan area.

Barry and I had been to the Memphis zoo once back in 1974.  I distinctly remember visiting the ape habitat, which contained a wall with windows where one could put his face within inches of a gorilla's face.  We did.

**Churches and stately old mansions lend traditional class to Memphis**

I was in Memphis at that time to watch the Tennessee Vols and the Maryland Terps square off in the Liberty Bowl.  I had made the trip down in my old '67 Plymouth Valiant, and Barry let me sleep on the sofa in his apartment.  Marcia had made the trip down separately with her family, who loved to frequent UT bowl games.  She stayed with her parents at a downtown hotel, but she and I and Barry and his date wandered all over Memphis seeing the sights.  I was particularly impressed with the airport—a highway ran right under a major

*A Slice of Tennessee*

runway. I'd never been run over by a jet airplane before. On Sunday morning we all attended First Baptist Church, where Barry attended while at school. I don't remember much about that experience except that they had a free lunch for college students afterward. As a college student, I was always looking for a free meal. By the way, the underdog Vols came from behind to defeat the Terps 7 to 3. And I arrived back in Nashville a few days later with the gas tank on empty and forty-five cents in my pocket.

Barry had had his own college-era experiences with scarce meals and trips made on pocket change. He had once thumbed a ride from Memphis to Martin, three hours away, to see our mutual buddy John Claxton at the University of Tennessee branch there. John and his wife-to-be Vickie set Barry up with a blind date, and the foursome took in a movie and then dinner at a local diner. John and Barry claimed they weren't very hungry as they ordered pie and coffee, while the girls ate a full meal. Actually they were both running low on money. I asked Barry if the girl was the typical blind date. "No," he replied, "she was a nice girl. But she did eat a lot." Barry arrived back in Memphis with less than a dollar to his name.

Now, more than three decades later, Barry was a geologist with a large multi-national corporation traveling to such exotic places as Nigeria and Kuwait on someone else's dime. And he and I were together again in Memphis, pedaling around Overton Park. I was particularly impressed with the many old stately mansions surrounding the Park. They were quite well-maintained. And except for a few improvements, the Park itself has remained undisturbed since its establishment in 1906. Therefore, local residents were understandably upset in the 1960's when construction plans revealed that Interstate 40 would cut a swath through the heart of the area. After much wrangling and even a U.S. Supreme Court ruling in 1971, the Department of Transportation backed down and routed I-40 over the existing I-240 route around the city. Apparently, citizens of Memphis wanted to preserve its traditional park. And why not? After all, Elvis gave his first public concert here in Overton Park Levitt Shell.

162

*Chapter 14   Jackson to Memphis:  Part II*

**No Interstate Highway through here!**

Speaking of Elvis, Barry and I were about to see another landmark of tradition as US 70 traversed over Union Avenue: Sun Studio.  Elvis got his start here.  When he auditioned at the (then) Sun Record Company, they asked him who he sounded like.  The eighteen-year-old aspiring singer said, "I don't sound like nobody!"  And the rest is history.  Elvis, it appears, was more interested in starting traditions than preserving them.  The studio is famous also for giving Johnny Cash, Roy Orbison, and Jerry Lee Lewis their start as well.  Huge photographs of all four are displayed on the side of the old brown brick corner-lot building.

There is so much to see and do in Memphis.  But the day was hot, humid.  Even Gatorade was having difficulty boosting our stamina.  I suggested to Barry that we make a beeline to the Old Bridge.  The Old Bridge is the same structure that took me across the Mississippi River for the first time in my life in 1961.  Dad was driving the family from our home in Florida to visit relatives in sunny Kansas. I still remember how imposing the bridge looked, how wide the river seemed.

**That's Elvis right behind my bicycle**

Barry and I were getting closer. We tipped our hats (or helmets) to Beale Street as our route passed it. B. B. King's Blues Club was on the corner.

*Chapter 14    Jackson to Memphis:  Part II*

Finding the bridge was not as easy as I thought it would be.  Interstate 55 actually crosses over the Old Bridge, as does Highway US 70.  There is a bicycle/pedestrian lane on either side, separated from the traffic lanes by a concrete Jersey barrier.  But we had to locate the right street leading to the right ramp to get there.  Our road kept T-ing into other roads.  I pulled out a huge map of Memphis trying to determine the best route just as two men pulled up to the stop sign.  Seeing our frowning faces, they offered to help.  They quickly pointed us toward Crump Blvd. and the Old Bridge.  I know some racial tensions still exist in Memphis, as elsewhere, but these two African-Americans, in the spirit of southern hospitality, gave us a friendly thumbs-up as they sped away.  Such instant moments of camaraderie had made this whole ride so rewarding.

The bridge was (thankfully) flat, not high and arched.  The bicycle/pedestrian lane was narrow but sufficient and even shady.  Seeing this structure, I couldn't help letting a single sob escape—I was within sight of my goal.

And so we pedaled, over the mighty muddy Mississippi River, always there, always impressive.  This river is the one that so captivated the fancy of a young riverboat pilot named Samuel Langhorne Clemens that he eventually took up his pen and, under the name Mark Twain, wrote of the adventures of young Huck Finn.  Generations ever since have stood in awe of young Huck's river.

Finally, there it was—right smack over the center of the river channel— "Welcome to Arkansas."  Barry and I stopped and took congratulatory pictures, just like two buddies having just scaled Mt. Everest.  The Mayor, Governor, and major news outlets were conspicuous by their absence.  Never mind—this ride never was about the flashy or the spectacular.  Nor was it about publicity or fame.  Or even about the Old Bridge or state lines.

*A Slice of Tennessee*

**It all began one rainy morning at the NC state line**

So what was it about? The smell of the sawmill in the rain outside Newport; memories from childhood in Knoxville of bike riding with another buddy to another bridge; the history exuding from a little stone stagecoach wayside inn that once hosted presidents and governors; a salute to the hospital that saved my life decades ago; reconnecting with family in Waverly; meeting new friends on the road, sampling southern hospitality all over. Truly, the journey *is* the destination.

And it was not quite over yet. I pedaled to the other side, just to plant my feet officially on Arkansas soil. Then I returned to the Great State of Tennessee and a ride of a few blocks where we would rendezvous with Jeff Jones and hot showers.

Speaking of rendezvous, while the ride was officially over, we still had more Memphis to sample—including eating some of those famous Rendezvous ribs and seeing some unbelievable ducks.

Chapter 14   Jackson to Memphis:  Part II

**Barry made it!!**

**I made it!!**

## A Slice of Tennessee

**41.70 miles for the day**

**586.15 miles total**

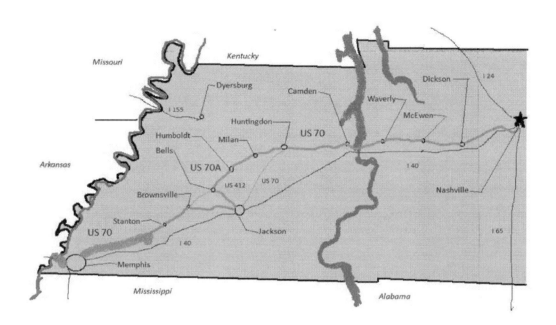

## Epilogue   The After-glow

Barry and I were standing outside the BP convenience store on Riverside Drive sipping on yet more Gatorade waiting for someone we'd never met to come pick us up. Alas, our ride was officially over. Or was it? For a few hours more we would be basking in the afterglow of the experience.

**after-glow  1 :** a glow remaining where a light has disappeared **2 :** a pleasant effect or feeling that lingers **after** something is done, experienced, or achieved.[1]

---

[1] Merriam-Webster online dictionary

*A Slice of Tennessee*

Yes, the ride was over, but after all, the journey itself *is* the destination. And there was still more journey to go. Jeff Jones soon arrived in his air conditioned minivan, loaded up two tired bicycles and two tired bicyclists and conveyed us to a Baptist Collegiate Ministries building a few blocks away. Jeff is the director of this student ministry organization for the University of Memphis, formerly Memphis State University. Jeff told us that not all alums are happy with the name change. Jeff is a Union University (Jackson, Tennessee) grad. He and his wife have four kids.

The BCM building had showers where we could clean up so as not to offend clientele later at the Peabody Hotel or Rendezvous Restaurant. The building is located adjacent to the campus of the University of Tennessee School of Medicine, where missionary Bill Wallace received his training many decades ago. Wallace, a native of Knoxville, served as a medical missionary to China and endured the Japanese invasion during World War II and the Communist takeover that occurred after the war. The Communist officials falsely accused him of espionage and confined him to prison, where they eventually beat him to death, to the sorrow of the many Chinese who loved the compassionate doctor. The BCM building has a library dedicated to this martyr's memory.

Refreshed and smelling a little sweeter, we climbed back into Jeff's van and headed toward the Peabody Hotel. Jeff proposed to his wife on the roof of the Peabody. They spent their wedding night in this hotel. The Peabody is an institution in Memphis, another classic example of the preservation of southern tradition. The cavernous lobby of this luxury hotel exudes elegance and includes a huge marble fountain which serves as the daytime playground for five ducks. The ducks live in their penthouse home, Duckingham Palace, at night. Every morning at 11:00 a.m. a "Duckmaster" in resplendent uniform with a fancy cane rolls out a red carpet from the elevator to the fountain. The ducks march out to their oversized birdbath to the background music of John Phillip Sousa's "King Cotton March." At exactly 5:00 p.m. the Duckmaster escorts the feathered celebrities back down the red carpet and up to their rooftop home. When a lady in the crowd of spectators asked the Duckmaster why he had to

*Epilogue: The After-glow*

wait until *exactly* 5:00 p.m., he replied, "Because the ducks do not expect to leave until five o'clock! Besides," he added, "it's a southern tradition."

The tradition began in the 1930's with two inebriated duck hunters sneaking their live decoys into the fountain as a joke. Within a few years hotel Bellman Edward Pembroke, a former animal trainer, began to march the ducks out to the fountain every day. He would continue in the capacity of Duckmaster for the next fifty years.

The current Duckmaster spent the minutes leading up to the hour profitably, befriending two young towheaded boys. He dubbed them "Honorary Duckmasters of the Day." They (and their mom) would accompany him and the ducks to their penthouse living quarters. Moments later the march began. The ducks waddled in step with Sousa, the Duckmasters striding along behind, careful to preserve the pomp and circumstance of the occasion. The southern tradition was preserved yet another day.

**John Phillip Sousa would be proud**

After witnessing the spectacle of the ducks, we needed to sample only one more Memphis tradition to make this trip complete: a rack of Charles Vergos's famous Rendezvous ribs. After pedaling ninety-six miles in two days, we were ready for a hearty meal. Rendezvous did not disappoint. The outside of the place didn't look like much. The entrance was accessed by a narrow alley. Once inside the front door, a narrow staircase led us hungry customers down to the underground, windowless dining area, where somewhat brusque waiters were serving the patrons. Memphis memorabilia adorned the walls, while paper placemats regaled the diner with the virtues of the establishment's dry rub ribs: "Not since Adam has a rib been this famous." "Hard as it is to believe, some folks don't eat pork ribs every chance they get." And my personal favorite, "About as far as a pig can go in this world." The ribs were not the fall-off-the-bone kind; you had to work and chew to get the meat off. It truly added to the culinary experience.

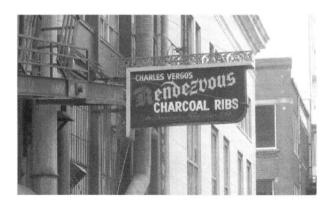

**Don't let the drab exterior fool you**

A retired student minister joined us for the meal: Charles Ray Griffin. Barry had recently reconnected with him and invited him to meet us at Rendezvous. This gracious servant of the Lord was thrilled to see Barry again, whom he knew as a Memphis State student in the 1970's. Charles and Jeff had not met previously but had much to talk about regarding student ministry.

*Epilogue: The After-glow*

Charles was thrilled that Barry had made contact after so many years. He thoroughly enjoyed the evening.

**That pig died for a worthy cause**

**Ministry forges strong relationships**

*A Slice of Tennessee*

So with bellies full of barbecue and hearts full of memories, we started back to Jackson. Jeff and I compared notes on our respective ministry experiences as he drove. He is a humble man and a mature minister. We discovered that our philosophies of ministry are quite similar. Old traditions, new friends—that's what this ride had been all about. And let's not forget old friends as well. Barry and I would drive on from Jackson to Nashville that night, where his parents had offered me lodging prior to returning home the next morning.

Tennessee is not universally beautiful and wholesome. It has its share of problems. I did encounter some negative facets of the state along the way. However, I ignored or downplayed these discoveries. My desire is not unlike that of the late Norman Rockwell or the late Louis Armstrong. Rockwell painted the wholesome view of Americana to the exclusion of anything negative or depressing. Rockwell did not believe our society was actually so pure and unspoiled; but he wanted to help people see the beauty and goodness around them and aspire to things higher and better. And old Satchmo was criticized over his song "What a Wonderful World." How could he sing such a song when war, racial tensions, poverty, etc., still plagued the world? His response was that this world could indeed be as he sang it if we would let it, if we exercised love instead of selfishness. He too saw beauty even in a marred world.

Likewise, my desire has been to help my fellow citizens see the evidence of the hand of the Lord even in an imperfect Tennessee, blessings He has given us richly to enjoy. Such blessings have made this slice of Tennessee a rare delicacy.

Now, if you'll excuse me, I believe I'll have another slice.

Made in the USA
Lexington, KY
05 November 2011